PRESENTED TO:

FROM:

DATE:

How to be a
father and live
to tell about it.

SURVIVAL
HANDBOOK
FOR DADS

BRUCE BICKEL AND STAN JANTZ

NASHVILLE,TENNESSEE
WWW.JCOUNTRYMAN.COM

COPYRIGHT © 2002 BY BRUCE BICKEL AND STAN JANTZ
PUBLISHED BY J. COUNTRYMAN®, A DIVISION OF THOMAS NELSON, INC.,
NASHVILLE, TENNESSEE 37214.

UNLESS OTHERWISE INDICATED, ALL SCRIPTURE QUOTATIONS IN THIS BOOK ARE FROM
THE HOLY BIBLE, NEW LIVING TRANSLATION (NLT) © 1996. USED BY PERMISSION
OF TYNDALE HOUSE PUBLISHERS, INC., WHEATON, ILL. ALL RIGHTS RESERVED.

THE NEW INTERNATIONAL VERSION OF THE BIBLE (NIV) © 1984 BY THE INTERNATIONAL
BIBLE SOCIETY. USED BY PERMISSION OF ZONDERVAN BIBLE PUBLISHERS.

DESIGNED BY: JACKSON DESIGN
BUDDY JACKSON [BJACKSON@BJACKSONDESIGN.COM], ART DIRECTOR;
LINDA BOURDEAUX, DESIGNER; ANGELA SMITH, PRODUCTION,
PROJECT EDITOR: KATHY BAKER

ISBN: 0-8499-9564-7

PRINTED AND BOUND IN THE UNITED STATES OF AMERICA

CONTENTS

INTRODUCTION

It isn't easy being a dad. We know. We—Bruce and Stan—have two kids apiece, and together we have logged more than eighty-eight years of dad-duty if you compute it on a per-child basis. We'll be the first to admit that the whole dad thing doesn't come naturally. Mostly it's on-the-job training. Our critters didn't come with an instructional manual, but we wouldn't have read it anyway. Hey, we're guys, just like you, and we don't need no stinking manuals. Right?

Actually, we could have used a little help along the way. Oh, sure, our wives had plenty of opinions about child safety and adolescent development—and they felt free to articulate their opinions. They even gave us reading assignments in books filled with psychobabble about pubescent social interaction issues. But that isn't the kind of information we needed. We're dads, not pediatric psychologists. We just wanted to make sure that we weren't doing something wrong that might leave our kids demented, disfigured, or disjointed.

WE WANT TO PROVIDE YOU WITH THE HANDBOOK WE NEVER HAD: A PRACTICAL, USER-FRIENDLY SURVIVAL GUIDE FOR MANEUVERING THROUGH THE MAZE OF FATHERHOOD.

We didn't care about birth-order neurosis or self-esteem psychosis. But we could have used a friendly "heads up" about the flammability of baby lotion, the number of hot dogs it takes for an eight-year-old to reach the regurgitation threshold at a monster truck rally, and the feasibility of implanting a global positioning transmitter in a teenager's backpack.

We want to provide you with the handbook we never had: a practical, user-friendly survival guide for maneuvering through the maze of fatherhood. You won't find any of those useless theories here. We're all about time-tested, proven techniques that have been used by dads through the centuries—tricks of the fathering trade if you will—that until this point have been passed down only by oral tradition.

This is no book for a Sigmund Freud or for any of those wimp psychologists who appear on *The Oprah Winfrey Show*. We're passing on survival tips for real-life, regular guys—the likes of Lance Armstrong, Bill Gates and Regis—guys like us and guys like you. Sure, we all come from different circumstances. We all don't have Lance's stamina, Bill's bucks, or Regis' panache, but we do have one thing in common: the brotherhood of fatherhood.

In the pages that follow we present methods that have served our predecessors well in the battle of wits between father and child. You'll find the absolute lack of esoteric theory and hypothesis refreshing. For your reading and comprehension convenience, we stick with analogies that you can relate to, things like sports and tools. But make no mistake about it. The father/child relationship must be taken seriously. It is no game. If you fail in your task of transforming your child into a successful, independent adult, you may jeopardize any prospects for your own comfortable retirement.

Bruce & Stan

P.S. After you have ~~appqax~~ appropriated the techniques in this handbook, pass it along to some fledgling father. It will be easy to find one. Just look for a guy with a dazed and befuddled expression on his face.

01

THE BEST LAID PLANS

There are many stereotypes out there about guys, some good, some not so good. An example of a stereotype that isn't so good is: Men are insensitive. A good stereotype would be something like: Men are good with directions.

As you can see from these two examples, just because a stereotype is considered good or bad doesn't mean that it's true. That's because all bad stereotypes are perpetuated by women, while all good stereotypes are perpetuated by men.

Why does this happen? Because women are constantly frustrated with men (we'll deal with this in a later chapter), and men just want to believe the best about themselves. Take the matter of directions. No self-respecting guy would ever stop and ask for directions, no matter how lost he is (and this includes taking his wife to the hospital to have their first baby).

The same thing goes for reading the directions to anything, especially something that requires assembly. It goes to the heart of a guy's manhood that he knows how to put together a swing set or a computer network without once looking at the instruction manual, even if it means having a bag full of nuts and bolts or a hundred yards of cable left over.

So we go through life doing our best to avoid directions. Is it any wonder, then, that we don't recognize those times when we really do need them? It's one thing to get lost on the way to a dinner party you don't want to attend in the first place, or to have extra pieces left over after assembling a bicycle. But when it comes to your offspring, you need a little more than instinct or manly confidence. You need a plan.

You certainly wouldn't want the builder of your dream home to fly by the seat of his pants. You don't want anything left out, and you don't want a pile of valuable building materials left over at the end. You want your house to come out exactly as the architect intended it.

Well, the same thing goes for your kids. As they grow up under your watchful care, you're like a builder. It's your job to follow the plans so your kids come out pretty close to the way the architect designed them (more about the architect in Section 1.1).

WHEN IT COMES TO YOUR OFFSPRING, YOU NEED A LITTLE MORE THAN INSTINCT OR MANLY CONFIDENCE. YOU NEED A PLAN.

We are the first ones to admit that the plans aren't always easy to follow. It takes months and years of studying and knowing your kid to uncover the intended design. But it's well worth it, which is why we are starting this *Survival Handbook for Dads* by encouraging you to start with a plan.

Real men tend to be "do it yourself" fanatics. Whether it is investing in stocks, repairing the car or installing a graphics card in the computer, we don't want to pay someone else to do what we could do ourselves. Doing it yourself is a way to save a few bucks (that could be better spent on green fees or sports memorabilia). More importantly, doing it yourself is a matter of pride. You don't even ask a stranger for directions, so why should you trust some physician you don't know to perform your appendectomy? How hard could it be to do it yourself?

There are a few situations, however, where you are required by law to hire a certified expert for guidance (such as that licensed engineer who refused to sign off on your plans to install a roof-top hot tub). When it comes to raising a kid, there is no law that requires you to consult a specialist, but common sense dictates that you shouldn't make this a do-it-yourself venture.

IF YOU FOLLOW YOUR OWN FATHERING INTUITIONS, YOUR CHILD MAY END UP IN JAIL, IN TRACTION OR IN THERAPY. IF SOMETHING LIKE THAT HAPPENS, YOU ARE GOING TO HAVE SOME MAJOR EXPLAINING TO DO.

If you follow your own fathering intuitions, your child may end up in jail, in traction or in therapy. Then you are going to have some major explaining to do. So, we suggest that you keep your fathering efforts within a framework that will assure the safety and sanity of your child. In other words, you can be responsible for building into your child's life, but you should follow a set of certified plans.

That brings us to the operative question: Whom are you going to rely upon as the architect for this construction project of immeasurable value?

> You could research the leadership skills of Attila the Hun. He certainly knew a thing or two about morale and discipline, but his techniques might be a bit severe for adolescents who are more concerned about acne than anarchy.

> You might prefer to pursue the ruminations that great philosopher, Yogi Berra. Every father needs the optimistic exhortation of Yogi's "It ain't over till it's over." Then again, Yogi also gave the admonition: "When you come to a fork in the road, take it."

Fortunately for you, we have discovered a book—thousands of years old—that contains the collected writings of approximately forty ancient authors. All of the wisdom a father needs can be found in the scrolls of those manuscripts (now available in paperback or bonded leather editions). We're talking about the Bible.

One of the writers was King Solomon, who is universally considered to be one of the wisest men who ever lived. He must have known a bit about fathering because he had hundreds of wives and concubines (which doesn't seem very wise to us). In the opening paragraph to the book of Proverbs, Solomon wrote:

> *Through these proverbs, people will receive instruction in discipline, good conduct, and doing what is right, just, and fair. These*

> proverbs will make the simpleminded clever.
> They will give knowledge and purpose to
> young people (Proverbs 1:3-4).

And the Bible also contains the teachings of Jesus who said:

> I will show you what it's like when someone
> comes to me, listens to my teaching, and
> then obeys me. It is like a person who
> builds a house on a strong foundation laid
> upon the underlying rock. When the
> floodwaters rise and break against the
> house, it stands firm because it is well
> built (Luke 6:47-48).

DON'T RELEGATE RAISING YOUR CHILD TO A DO-IT-YOURSELF PROJECT. YOUR SELF-DIRECTED EFFORTS MIGHT LEAVE YOU LOOKING MORE LIKE YOGI BEAR THAN YOGI BERRA. AND THEN YOUR CHILD WOULD END UP BEING THE BOO-BOO.

Don't relegate raising your child to a do-it-yourself project. You might be well intentioned, but your self-directed efforts might leave you looking more like Yogi Bear than Yogi Berra. And then your child would end up being the Boo-Boo. For once in your life, resist the do-it-yourself temptation. Read the blueprint for fathering that is set forth in the Bible. You can be the builder of your child's life, but let God be the architect. After all, God knows what it takes to be a dad. That's why he is called our heavenly Father.

It doesn't take long for most dads to develop ideas about who or what their kids are going to become. This is especially true of boys. A proud papa will notice the way his three-month-old waves his right arm and conclude that he's got the makings of an NFL quarterback.

With girls, the signals are more subtle. Your two-year-old daughter may be able to sing her nursery rhymes in perfect pitch, but that doesn't mean she's going to be the next Charlotte Church.

It's natural to want your kids to achieve greatness and success, but resist the temptation to overreact to specific talents and tendencies.

However, don't ignore your child's gifts and talents either. If your son or daughter excels in sports or music, give them every opportunity to develop the skills and knowledge needed to succeed, even if they never go farther than Pee Wee football or the junior high glee club. If your kid shows a knack for putting stuff together, buy a LEGO set. If junior would rather read than throw a pass, don't lament a lost sports career; bring home more books.

What do you want your kid to look like in the end? Is it an image you've always had in your mind—whether or not it's realistic—or is it a picture that's developed from the strengths and unique abilities of your son or daughter? Your mental image may or may not be true, but the real picture will eventually come into focus—as long as you give it time to develop.

1.3 ATTENTION TO DETAIL

Details are important. You wouldn't build a cabinet without knobs on the drawers. You wouldn't order a new computer for your home office but forget the monitor. And you wouldn't restore a classic '57 Corvette and use hubcaps off a '98 Hyundai. You've got to give attention to the details so that nothing is overlooked.

The same principle applies to raising children. As a dad, you can't focus on one aspect of your child's character to the exclusion of others. For example, athletic development is important, but you can't ignore your child's intelligence (if for no other reason than to comprehend the terms of that multi-year pro sports contract you'll negotiate after your kid graduates from college).

We know you've got a lot on your mind (such as figuring out how you will spend your fifteen percent agent's fee off your child's multi-year pro sports contract). So, we won't burden you with a long list of character traits that you should instill in your child. We'll boil it down to four categories:

1. Mental: You kid has a brain. Make sure it gets used.

2. Physical: It is not necessary that your child become an Olympic contender, but his or her favorite position shouldn't be in the La-Z-Boy in front of the television. (That place should be reserved for you.)

3. Social: Interpersonal relationships are an

important part of life. Skills in that area aren't developed by sitting alone in a room with a game console or staring into a computer screen. (And chat rooms and Instant Messenger don't count because your child won't learn the nuances of body language or the fine art of facial expressions.)

4. Spiritual: We aren't talking about the rules, regulations, and rituals of a stale religion. No kid is interested in that (and neither is any adult). But your child should be very familiar with God—in a context other than cursing.

It is your dadly duty to give attention to these four details. Skip any one of them, and you run the risk that your child will grow up to be a Hyundai instead of a classic Corvette.

THE LONG AND SHORT OF IT

You might be intimidated at the prospects of devising a grand design for your child's entire life. Don't be. Like eating an elephant, your kid's life can be chewed up one bite at a time. Consider short-term goals as well as long-term objectives. For example:

AREA OF LIFE	SHORT-TERM GOAL	LONG-TERM OBJECTIVE
mental	able to budget and manage a modest allowance	able to invest your modest retirement account
physical	strong enough to lift his or her own weight	strong enough to lift your weight (so your child will be physically able to move you from the couch to your bed without waking you)
social	one or two good friends	at least one friend in each of the following occupations: medicine, law, computer programming, and plumbing
spiritual	an awareness of other religious and respect for other faiths	at least one good Catholic connection who can finagle tickets for you to attend a football game at Notre Dame

There's something very important you should know about all your plans to nurture a healthy, happy, smart, successful kid: they will change. That's not to say that your kid won't be healthy, happy, smart, and successful. It's just that he or she will probably get there despite your best laid plans, not because of them.

The reason is that kids don't necessarily follow your advice to do things a certain way, unless it involves incentives. For example, if you tell your son to practice the piano for thirty minutes a day (because you dream about him becoming a concert pianist), your advice will go unheeded. But if you tell your little Van Cliburn that you will let him play with his Game Boy for every minute he practices the piano, then he is well on his way to a Carnegie Hall debut by the age of twelve.

Because kids tend to go their own way rather than yours, you will find yourself constantly changing your plans and making adjustments along the way. Don't worry. These changes show wisdom rather than weakness, especially since the blueprints you develop for your kids tend to be more idealistic than realistic.

Early on, your plans for your kids' well being and success are based on your

EARLY ON, YOUR PLANS FOR YOUR KIDS' WELL BEING AND SUCCESS ARE BASED ON YOUR OWN PREFERENCES AND PERSONALITY. BUT AS YOU GET TO KNOW YOUR CHILDREN MORE, YOU WILL FIND THAT YOUR PLANS WILL BE BASED MORE ON THEIR PREFERENCES AND PERSONALITIES.

own preferences and personality. But as you get to know your children more and more (hint: this involves spending lots of time with them from day one, and it never stops), you will find that your plans will be based more on their preferences and personalities.

In keeping with our metaphor of God as the architect and dad as the builder, you need to make these adjustments in the same way a good homebuilder adapts to the preferences and personalities of the people who will eventually occupy the house, not the other way around. Remember, your kids—not you—are the ones who live their lives. About all you can hope for is to provide opportunities as you guide them along their way.

You know what? In the end that's not a bad way to go, and it's going to be more satisfying than you can imagine.

1.5 THE BEST LAID PLANS

Since this book is a survival handbook for dads, we think it is appropriate to quote from the U. S. Army's Field Service Regulations for military operations:

> The final test of a plan is its execution.

That principal certainly applies to dads. Planning is important, but it doesn't mean anything if there is no follow through. You've got to put the plan into action. But that's the tricky part because the performance of a plan is always more difficult than the design phase. As military strategist James F. Hollingsworth said:

> Any fool can write a plan. It's the execution that gets you all screwed up.

If you're like most guys—and we think you are—you'll be tempted to spend a great deal of time developing a plan for raising your children. Upon its completion, there will be an equally excessive duration in which you admire your plan and marvel at the intricacies of your design. By the time you get around to get ready to begin to prepare for the implementation of the plan, your child will be looking at brochures for your nursing home.

Don't spend so much time planning to be a good dad that you miss the opportunity for actually being a good dad. And don't forget that all the planning in the world won't mean a thing unless you have complete faith that the plans you are following have been designed by an architect you can trust completely.

Commit your work to the Lord, and then your plans will succeed (Proverbs 16:3).

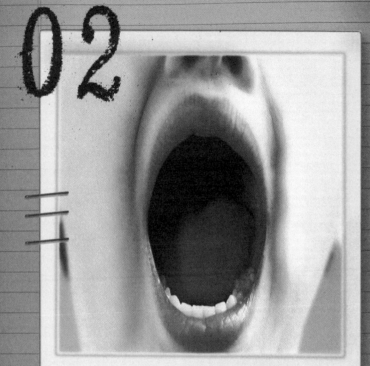

02

GROWING PAINS

2.0 LOOK AT THAT KID GROW

As guys, we enjoy a sense of accomplishment that comes from seeing a project progress from start to finish. It could be something as complicated as constructing a second-story loft in the cabin at the lake. Or, it could be as simple as creating a tower of fifteen Cheetos stacked on top of each other. There is sheer delight in each feat.

A dad gets a similar feeling watching his child grow up. With the passage of each developmental stage—beginning at diapers and progressing to a diploma and beyond—there is pride and a sense of achievement.

Each dad takes a little credit for the success of his progeny's progression. We have to affirmatively take this credit because no one—especially the child or the mother—will give us much recognition for our participation in the process. But our sense of pride is not so much about us and our influence and involvement in our child's development. It is more about our child's personal accomplishment of maturity. Somehow, what was once a blob of squalling flesh has now become a real person, or at least a reasonable facsimile thereof. And it is to the kid's credit that this happened despite Dad's influence and involvement.

SOMEHOW, WHAT WAS ONCE A BLOB OF SQUALLING FLESH HAS NOW BECOME A REAL PERSON, OR AT LEAST A REASONABLE FACSIMILE THEREOF. AND IT IS TO THE KID'S CREDIT THAT THIS HAPPENED DESPITE DAD'S INFLUENCE AND INVOLVEMENT.

The development of your child won't happen all at once, but it doesn't proceed in a steady progression either. It goes in spurts. And the growth can't always be gauged with a tape measure or a bathroom scale. Sometimes the advancement is cerebral in nature (but this kind may be undetected because it is often accompanied by an obnoxious attitude).

In this chapter we will alert you to the changes that your child will undergo as part of the natural progression from infant to adult. You need to be warned so that you can be ready. You want to be ready because you'll want to claim credit whenever possible. Any you'll want to be ready because you'll want to avoid blame whenever necessary. But most of all, you'll want to be ready because you'll be sorry if you miss it.

The entire process of giving birth is one of the most incredible, amazing, and happy occasions you will ever experience. Of course, as a dad, you can say this because you aren't the one giving birth. Your wife has a different perspective, generally defined by pain. For her, the words incredible, amazing, and happy can be modified to incredibly painful, amazingly difficult, and I'm happy it's over!

That's not to say that you won't be under your own stress. In fact, as a dad you will endure emotional trauma that's probably more difficult to handle than mere physical pain. (Warning: your wife will not agree with this, so it's wise not to bring it up.)

As a public service for any dad who a) has never witnessed the birth of a child; or b) passed out at the birth of your last kid, here is a list of what you will likely experience:

PANIC
The feeling you will have when your wife says, "I think my water just broke."

ADRENALINE RUSH
This will happen when you drive to the hospital at death-defying speeds, and then realize you left your wife at home.

REJECTION
Your beautiful wife, who has been so appreciative of the way you have been treating her during her pregnancy, will turn into another creature during labor (think Linda Blair in *The Exorcist*).

SHOCK

If you are privileged to actually witness the birth of your baby, you need to prepare yourself for what you'll encounter. Forget images of a Gerber baby, all soft and cuddly. The first thing you will see is a quivering, wrinkly creature—and that's just your mother-in-law waiting outside! Your kid will be much worse.

CONTRACTIONS

These aren't physical reflexes, but rather something that starts happening to your bank account the minute you bring your baby home from the hospital and start feeding, clothing, and cleaning up after him or her. (Note: contractions don't stop until, well, actually they never stop.)

The good news is that all of these negative things (except for the contractions) will fade away. Replacing them will be positive feelings of joy, wonder, and thankfulness, mainly because that wrinkled prune you saw is your kid, and there's nothing more beautiful in the world.

The phrase "disposable diaper" has a double meaning:

a) the diaper can be discarded after it has been used for its intended purpose; and

b) the price of those absorbent devices can effectively dispose of your income.

Due to the financial cost and the caustic fumes, you will be anxious for your toddler to advance from Pampers to the porcelain potty, but it won't happen fast enough for you. You'll be tempted to vent your frustration on your child, but resist the urge strap your kid on the toilet seat with a roll of duct tape.

It has been a long time since you were a carpet crawler yourself, so we'll remind you of this universal truth: toddlers are afraid of toilets. To them, the toilet is a dangerous and deadly device. Think about it from their perspective:

> The thing is twice as big as they are. You'd be afraid of a toilet too if it was nine feet high and six feet wide, holding 107 gallons of water, with a flushing capacity that could suck you under faster than you could swim.

> Your child has seen your pained expression with your body doubled over in agony as you headed toward the bathroom.

> Although you didn't know it, your toddler

has heard your agonizing grunts and groans from behind the bathroom door.

And perhaps most frightening of all, your child has suffered the effects of the noxious odors that emanated from the bathroom as you left. Those toxic fumes were enough to make any child's eyes water and throat constrict.

With that kind of preliminary exposure to the bathroom, is it any wonder that your child is deathly afraid of it?

If you are serious about accelerating your child's toilet training, you are going to have to make the toilet your child's friend. This will only happen if you take the following steps: First, you will have to decorate the toilet like a prop from Sesame Street. (We suggest that you try to simulate the trashcan of Oscar the Grouch, but tell your kid that Oscar is on vacation.) Second, when you have to use the facility, don't use the one in your house; go to your neighbor's.

CLUES YOU CAN USE

Guys tend to be oblivious to much of what changes in the world around them. We are sorry to say it so bluntly, but we have to be honest about it. You didn't notice when your wife changed her hairstyle, and you haven't noticed that your physique slipped from sexy to slouchy more than a decade ago.

AGE (IN YEARS)	EYES
0-1	unfocused & unaligned
2-5	they won't take their eyes off of you (it's creepy)
6-12	they will never look directly at you (it's creepy)
13-19	unfocused & unaligned (usually due to lack of sleep or overexposure to television or computer screens)

We don't want you to be equally oblivious to your child's development. The chart below will help you identify your child's growth stage by simply monitoring eye movement, hand action and speech patterns.

HANDS	VERBAL SKILLS
flailing & uncoordinated but they can't do any damage	incoherent
fingers in the orifices of the mouth, nose, or ears	monosyllabic commands
flailing & uncoordinated, and they break everything they touch	incessant questions in no logical pattern
fingers in mouth (usually due to constant eating but never related to oral hygiene)	incoherent, monosyllabic commands in no logical pattern

2.3 KID IN A BARREL

Dr. James Dobson once gave some advice on how to handle teenagers. He suggested that when a kid reaches the age of thirteen, you should simply seal him or her in a wooden barrel, leaving an opening on top just large enough for food and other essentials, such as vast quantities of hair gel.

We immediately liked this idea and decided to try it on our own kids rather than run the risk of actually trying to manage them through those minefield years that last from the beginning of junior high to high school graduation.

When someone (one of our teenagers) pointed out that Dr. Dobson was merely using hyperbole to make the point that raising teenagers is not for the faint of heart, the first thing we did was to look up the word "hyperbole." (We were disappointed to learn that it is "an exaggerated statement used for effect and not meant to be taken literally.") Then we searched our bookshelves for anything by Dr. Dobson that might help us and found *Parenting Isn't For Cowards*. The title of the book alone was enough to set us into a panic. (This initial feeling quickly subsided and was replaced by a general state of terror.)

Now that our kids are safely through the teenage years and on to the even more terrifying state of college and early adulthood (see the next section), we can safely and confidently say that for us the teenage years weren't as bad as we thought they would be. They were worse (just kidding).

Seriously, there's nothing to be afraid of, as long as you've got your wits about you—along with your night vision binoculars, jumper cables, medical emergency kit, and the phone number for 911.

THERE'S NOTHING TO BE AFRAID OF, AS LONG AS YOU'VE GOT YOUR WITS ABOUT YOU—ALONG WITH YOUR NIGHT VISION BINOCULARS, JUMPER CABLES, MEDICAL EMERGENCY KIT, AND THE PHONE NUMBER FOR 911.

Oh, and it wouldn't hurt to learn from our experience. As a wise person once said, you won't live long enough to make all the mistakes yourself, so learn from the mistakes of others. Since we've made more than our share of mistakes, we think we can save you a lifetime of grief (okay, it will only seem like a lifetime). So, whether you are now or will someday be the father of at least one teenager, following are ten things we learned about raising teenagers (and lived to tell about it).

37

TEN THINGS TO KNOW ABOUT RAISING TEENAGERS

1. Teenager is simply another word for alien. Sometime during your child's twelfth year, a strange creature will swap bodies with your kid; and stick around another six or seven years.

2. You will know your son has become a teenager when his body emits odors not unlike those found near a New Jersey landfill.

3. To counteract this olfactory problem, your teenage son will ask you to buy him industrial-size containers of cologne, deodorant, and acne medicine. Do not deny his requests.

4. Teenage girls don't have the same odor challenge as boys, but they will have a sudden desire to apply large quantities of body lotions and face paint that will set them apart from every other person except their friends and the current favorite singing sensation.

5. Teenagers generally develop their own, like, vocabulary, you know, and their own way of talking. Don't be alarmed. This language can be learned as long as you hang around your teenagers and their friends (out of sight, of course).

6. Your teenager probably will develop ideas and opinions different from yours. Again, don't panic. As long as these ideas don't involve illegal activities or disgusting habits, encourage your kids to think for themselves. Hey, you never know, you might learn something.

7. Transportation will become a big issue for your teenager—namely any transportation that doesn't involve you. Don't take this personally. Put yourself in your kid's shoes; it's hard to look cool driving with your dad in his 1982 Dodge Diplomat. If your teenager does ask you for a ride, don't be offended when she asks you to drop her off a block away from her destination.

8. Once your teenager starts driving, we have just two pieces of advice: Pray like you've never prayed before, and let him drive your Dodge Diplomat. Prayer always helps, and at this point a few more dents and spills won't hurt the resale value of your car.

9. Also, your driving teenager will spend even more time away from home. In order to keep up with your teenager's activities, ask a lot of questions and realize that most of the answers are only partially true.

10. Above all, let your teenagers know that you trust them. Of course, they must earn your trust, but once they've earned it, give them more rope. Trust us, a teenager who is trusted is more likely to be responsible than one whose parents constantly question them.

As your child progresses through each developmental stage, you'll have to make some major adjustments to your fathering skills and styles. The peek-a-boo games that kids love when they are babies will be very annoying to them when they are in junior high school. And the warden-like approach that you used with your teenager on issues such as curfew won't work when your kid lives in a dorm at college (unless you moonlight as a campus security guard).

UNTIL THIS POINT, YOU HAVE BEEN A HANDS-ON PARENT. NOW IT'S TIME TO CONSIDER YOURSELF AS AN OUTSIDE CONSULTANT.

When your child makes the move from high school to college, the biggest adjustment may be your responsibility. This stage marks your student's move into adulthood. Until this point, you have been a hands-on parent. Now it's time to consider yourself as an outside consultant. This is the tricky part. Your child will have a newfound sense of independence that will run contrary to any sense of obligation or accountability to you.

It won't be easy to get information out of your college student. Your inquiries will be misconstrued as interrogations. Your expressions of interest will be viewed as an intrusion. If you want information about what your kid is doing, you can get it, but you'll have to be sneaky about it:

> Make sure your kid thinks you're just
> "checking in" instead of "checking up."
> Email is great in this regard (even if your

college student still lives in the bedroom down the hall from yours). Tell your child what is going on in your life and with the other members of the family. Maybe you'll get lucky and receive a reply.

Learn to listen instead of lecture. (Why do you think that God gave you two ears but only one mouth? That was a facial design intended for the dad of a college student.)

Give advice only when asked. This may be the hardest technique for you to learn. Yes, you have lots of life experience, but allow your son or daughter a chance to get some of their own.

Your college student will hate it if you ask a lot of questions (that litany of who, what, when, and so forth is particularly offensive). If you must do it, then tell your kid that these questions are for the purpose of praying, not prying. But don't immediately fold your hands and close your eyes, because you might get sucker punched.

Nothing grows without pain or effort. It's true in nature, and it's true in your family. There's physical growth, which is going to happen whether you like it or not (such as when your little girl turns into a young woman overnight, and suddenly a bunch of hairy young men with exploding hormones come knocking at your door).

Then there's the growth in your kids that you can't really see, but it's just as real, and in many ways even more important. This kind of intangible growth of mind, heart, and soul can also be more painful, especially if you and your kids try to go it alone. You can't live their lives for them, of course, but you can help them draw their nourishment from the truth about God and His love.

It won't happen overnight, but your children will grow in the knowledge and love of God, especially if they see you doing the same thing.

> *Let your roots grow down into him and draw up nourishment from him, so you will grow in faith, strong and vigorous in the truth you were taught. Let your lives overflow with thanksgiving for all he has done (Colossians 2:7).*

03

THE ORGANIZED DAD

Ever since the beginning of time, men have felt the need to get organized by writing stuff down. The problem is that once a guy writes something down, he can't always find it. This tendency started very early in our history:

Eve: Adam, did you finish naming the animals like God asked you to?
Adam: I almost finished, but then I lost my list.
Eve: What happened?
Adam: Well, I wrote the names on sheepskin, but then something spooked the sheep. I can't finish naming the animals until my list returns.

Nowadays we don't have to write our lists and appointments down on sheepskin; we've got all kinds of paper and—wonder of wonders—those marvelous personal digital assistants to assist us in the storage of everyday knowledge and long-term memory.

Of course, we all know that making lists isn't the real issue for guys. It's retrieving those important items and dates—and then actually following through on them—that makes the difference.

Getting organized is especially critical for us dads, mainly because our kids happen to believe that their dad does what he says. The last thing you want to do is to let them down because you forgot to do something you said you would do.

If you've messed up in this area, don't be too hard on yourself. Hey, we've all been there. But we can do better. That's why we want to take this chapter to look at some creative ways dads can get organized for the benefit of their kids.

3.1 SCHEDULE YOURSELF

(BEFORE SOMEONE ELSE DOES)

There's lots going on in your life. You are a busy guy. You are important. People depend on you. You know these things about yourself, but here is something you probably don't know—what to put first.

Many dads make the disastrous mistake of failing to schedule the priorities of life. They get so busy doing many trivial things that they don't have time for the few important things. Don't let this happen to you. Figure out what is important, plan time for those big things, and then work the small stuff into the time that's left over.

Consider that your life is like a big bucket. You have to fill your "bucket" with:

BIG ROCKS

These would be the things that are most important to you, like your children. Your wife is another big rock (notice that we didn't say millstone). Because you depend upon an income, your job also qualifies in this category.

SMALL STONES

These are commitments and relationships that aren't as big as the rocks, but they are still very important. They might include your close friends and your involvement at church or in some community organizations.

SAND

These are the myriad of things you do that won't make a bit of difference five years from now. They include those obligations that you got yourself into just because you didn't say "no" when you were asked.

Here is where we are going with this. If you start by filling your bucket to the top with sand, there will be no room available for the rocks and stones. You've got to begin by filling your bucket with the rocks. The most important things in your life go into the bucket first. Then, you can still fit quite a few small stones into the bucket (although it may require a little shaking). After the rocks and the stones are in, there will still be room for some sand in the gaps and crevices.

Learn to schedule your life around the important things. Put the rocks in first.

(A word of caution: Bruce is a lawyer, so he is insisting that we remind you that this bucket thing is an analogy. Bruce doesn't want us to be sued by some dimwit dad who put sand in his crevices.)

HOW TO AVOID LOSING YOUR KID

At any age, your kid will be relatively mobile. We think it has something to do with Newton's Third Law of Displacement: "A thing with legs tends to remain in motion." That means your kid will move from where you placed it. Count on it.

There are two things you need to remember about losing a kid:

1: This is a very bad thing. Don't let it happen. Your credibility and reputation as a great dad will be in jeopardy. Guys who are considered to be great dads tend to know at least the general geographic proximity of their kids.

2: Regardless of how it happened, somehow losing a kid is always the dad's fault. Don't think that you can talk your way out of this one.

Unfortunately, no single skill or device is effective at all ages of your child. (No, this isn't like romance where you can always count on a splash of Old Spice to work its wonders on your wife.) You are going to have to develop techniques commensurate with your child's progressive propensity of propulsion:

AS AN INFANT

They don't travel much at this stage. They just lie there. But it is easy to get your child mixed up with someone else's baby. Let's face it. No matter what your wife says, all kids at this age look alike. (Don't ever express this opinion to your wife!) We

suggest a few strategically placed markings with a
Sharpie pen.

AS A TODDLER
Kids at this stage never stay still. They are in a
constant state of exploration. Some parents use a
leash. We recommend against this technique because it
seems rather demeaning to the child. Our solution is
portable chain link fencing.

AS AN ADOLESCENT
Bribery works best. You'll have to determine if the
best bribe is junk food, video games, or sports.
Whatever it is, discover your child's weakness, and
exploit it to your advantage.

AS A TEENAGER
At this stage, you can't restrain them from driving
away, but you can control the distance that they
travel. The fuel tank in your car should never
contain more then one gallon of gasoline. Your
"search radius" will be determined by your car's fuel
efficiency.

Never losing your kid won't make you a good dad.
But you are less likely to lose your kid if you are a
good dad. That's the best technique for keeping your
child near you: be a good dad.

3.2 DATES AND EVENTS

YOU DON'T WANT TO MISS

Let's face it. Knowing which dates and events are important for a dad isn't all that hard. You know what they are, and we know what they are, so let's make a list of the most important days every dad should keep—without fail. Get your trusty PDA (or your daily planner if you're still into pen and paper) and log these in. You won't regret it.

YOUR WIFE'S BIRTHDAY AND YOUR ANNIVERSARY

These dates are priority number one. Your wife and your marriage come first, and your kids need to know that (so does your wife).

YOUR KIDS' BIRTHDAYS

You might be at the stage in life when you are trying to forget your own birthdays, but your kids can't wait for theirs. Never miss these even after your kids are out of the nest.

ANY SPECIAL EVENT INVOLVING YOUR KIDS

These include recitals, games, award ceremonies, church events, and anything you can think of to make your kids feel special. You're not going to make all the events, but shoot for most of them. You have no idea how much your presence (not necessarily your presents) means to your kids.

CHURCH

There are no heavenly brownie points for perfect church attendance, but earthly benefits of regularly attending a local church with your family are enormous. Don't miss out on the chance to grow spiritually with your wife and kids.

HOLIDAYS

We've got holidays for just about everything these days, but that doesn't diminish the fact that holidays were originally holy days set apart to recognize God's faithfulness. This still applies to special days like Easter and Christmas, but you can turn other holidays like Memorial Day and Labor Day into opportunities to teach your kids about God's goodness all the time.

SURPRISE DAYS

One of the great things about being a dad is that you can make stuff up—like special events for no reason at all. Imagine the joy of a child who gets to spend a school day with dad. Imagine the joy of your child.

As any good salesman can tell you, contacts are everything. You already know this, and whether it is on your computer, in your daily planner, or locked in the recesses of your mental memory, you have your own list of contacts: your friends, your work associates, your stockbroker, your bookie and your bail bondsman.

Your kid isn't any different. Your child has his or her own set of contacts—those friends who are your kid's confidants and co-conspirators. These are the ones you have to know and worry about.

Regardless of the age of your child, there are three friends in the contact group that you need to identify and dispose of. We'll help you with the identification process, but you'll need to come up with the disposal techniques on your own.

THE INSTIGATOR

This is the kid who always comes up with the foolish ideas for activities that end up involving blood, handcuffs, or an embarrassing photograph in the local newspaper. If you want to reduce your medical and legal expenses, weed this kid out of your child's contacts.

THE HYPOCRITE

You'll like this kid at first. In fact, of all your child's friends, this kid will be your favorite. Don't get sucked into the vortex of deceit. This kid is two-faced. When he or she is around you, you'll hear nothing but compliments and expressions of appreciation. As soon as you leave the room, you'll be the target of this kid's ridicule. If you plan on having any credibility with your child, the hypocrite must be eliminated.

THE DOOFUS

This kid isn't bad, but neither are slugs and snails. The fault of the doofus is that he or she has no ambition in life. The doofus won't inspire your child to greatness. Instead, the doofus will drag your child down to the depths of mediocrity. You'll have to delay any plans for retirement if your child spends too much time with the doofus.

You can only rid your child's life of these negative influences if you know your child's friends. (Note: those remote miniature video cameras can be purchased on the Internet.)

But what if your kid is the problem child in the group? That's great because the other kids will be a positive influence on your child. Let's face it. if you've got the instigator, the hypocrite, or the doofus, then some other dad has to worry about your child.

3.4 GOTTA HAVE A SYSTEM THAT WORKS

We've done our best to emphasize the importance for a dad to be organized. If you can't keep track of the important details, you might as well surrender your fathering credentials. (Ouch!)

Some dads make the mistake of using a handheld computing device for organizational purposes. In our humble (but correct) opinion, these PDAs are ineffective for the following reasons:

Too Costly: Ranging in price from $100 to $500, this is too much money to spend on a device that could be replaced by a pencil and a piece of paper. If you don't think so, then you haven't made any college tuition payments yet.

Too Technical: The digital readout on your VCR is still flashing "12:00." What makes you think that you can master the technical intricacies of a PDA?

Too Cliche: Everybody has one. Imagine the admiring looks you'll receive at your next meeting when everyone opens their briefcase for their PDAs and you simply reach into your shirt pocket for a pen and a pad of sticky notes.

If you use scraps of paper for your organizational mechanisms, then you must decide where to collect them. Most novices choose the refrigerator door. This is a rookie mistake. Anything you put on the refrigerator will soon be covered by layers of shopping lists, school notices, and that photo of you hugging your mother-in-law.

The best place to post your important notes is in your bathroom. This is where you spend a lot of time and are always looking for something to read.

3.5 TIME FOR NOTHING

It's important to schedule and to plan and to be a responsible dad. It takes effort to guide your kids in an organized fashion, to do all you can to help them develop into loving, responsible adults.

You should never get tired of doing the right thing, but sometimes you have to throw your schedule to the wind and forget about being the Organized Dad. We're not talking about long stretches of irresponsibility, but rather short bursts of fun where you and your kids do, well, nothing.

The thing is, life is too short to miss out on the ordinary, everyday experiences that come when nothing is planned. It takes time to do nothing, but it's worth every minute.

> *Lord, remind me how brief my time on earth will be (Psalm 39:4).*

04

THE GAME OF LIFE

The same person who gave you this book might have criticized you in the past for knowing more about your favorite athlete than about your own child. That person obviously doesn't understand the appeal of sports statistics or the uselessness of a child's middle name.

Any self-respecting male knows the number of home runs hit by Hank Aaron (715) or the total passing yards of Joe Montana (40,551), or the first MVP of the WNBA (Cynthia Cooper, Houston Comets). That kind of trivia comes up all of the time in everyday conversation. But when was the last time that you used your child's middle name?

YOU AREN'T JUST A DAD. YOU ARE A COACH, A MENTOR, A TRAINER, AND THE OWNER OF THE FRANCHISE. YOUR CHILD IS THE YOUNG RECRUIT WITH SUPERSTAR POTENTIAL.

If you have been feeling guilty that you're more interested in sports than in fathering, you just need to tweak your perspective a bit. Don't view your role as a father as some sort of biological burden. Instead, think of your relationship with your child in a sports context. You aren't just a dad. You are a coach, a mentor, a trainer, and the owner of the franchise. Your child is the young recruit with superstar potential.

You can also gain a fresh perspective on your role as a dad by thinking of yourself as an athlete. World-class competitors take a holistic approach to life. They keep their mind, body, and spirit in top shape. Perhaps you already have a miniature plastic

trophy that is inscribed "World's Greatest Dad."
Well, it's time you get into the right physical,
mental, and spiritual shape to be deserving of such
an award.

In the next few pages, will give you some tips for
how to play the game of fatherhood. We'll be making
our points in sports metaphors. To make yourself
comfortable and get in the right frame of mind, you
might want to sit on the couch with the remote
control and a bag of potato chips by your side. Or,
slip on your cleats and go run a few wind sprints
before reading.

4.1 COACH DAD

For guys, no occupation is more respected than coaching. Say what you will about managing directors, corporate vice presidents, or CEOs, the status of a coach beats them all.

That's because a coach—particularly a successful coach—incorporates all the positive and redeeming qualities guys dream about having: boss, motivator, strategist, and teacher. And to top it all off, a coach gets to order around athletes who could either squash him like a bug or run circles around him athletically (and this includes the female athletes).

WHETHER YOU HAVE A TEAM OF ONE OR ENOUGH KIDS TO START YOUR OWN BASKETBALL TEAM, YOUR GREATEST CALLING AS COACH DAD IS TO BRING OUT THE BEST IN YOUR KIDS.

Of course, there's a lot more to coaching that simply telling people what to do. It's about encouraging people to do more than they think they are capable of doing. It's about building a team of players who can accomplish more together than they can as individuals. It's about setting and reaching goals. Hey, come to think of it, being a coach is a lot like being a dad.

Think about it. As a dad, your job is to teach and train and encourage your kids. Whether you have a team of one or enough kids to start your own basketball team, your greatest calling as Coach Dad is to bring out the best in your kids.

And here's something else about coaching. When the team wins, it's the team members who do the celebrating, not the coach. You'll never see the coach appear in those ads where the star athlete gets to go to Disney World, and that's the way it should be. Coaches don't grab the spotlight; they point it at the team. Coach Dad doesn't take the glory; he directs it to his kids.

Tiger Woods is an accomplished golfer (how is that for an understatement), but he still practices his putting. Kobe Bryant has logged quite a few hours on the hardwood, but he still shoots free throws in his spare time. Mia Hamm is master of the soccer ball, but she still runs the drop kick drills. No matter how good you get, you don't stay good unless you keep practicing the basics.

As a dad, you've got a few basics that you can't ignore. Don't be so intent on developing the character of your child that you forget about the fundamentals of fathering. Here is a short list of the skills drills for dads:

LISTENING

All dads can hear their kids, but a really great dad listens to his. Don't think that you can get away with listening while you simultaneously read the newspaper or watch TV. That's called multi-tasking, and it is a sign to your kid that he or she is not worthy of your full attention. Listening involves your eyes as well as your ears.

AFFECTION

Unless your ancestors were Italian, you might not have experienced much hugging in your household when you were a child. But the era of Vince Lombardi has been supplanted by the age of Phil Jackson. It is now okay for a guy to show emotion. If you aren't comfortable with it, get over it. Your kid needs to be convinced of your love and affection, and nothing says it better than an upper torso squeeze that will pop a few vertebrae.

DISCIPLINE

You might think that this comes naturally, but the punishment that you dish out on the spur of the moment probably isn't very good. There is an art to discipline (just ask any prison warden). If it is too mild, then it won't be effective. But it shouldn't be excessive either. Effective discipline requires that you know your child. Deprivation only works if you know what your child doesn't want to lose. The best discipline is the result of creativity and forethought.

TEMPERAMENT

The best fathers are dependable. Volatility is not an admirable trait for dads. You need to make sure that your character is consistent and that your moods are controlled.

If Tiger, Kobe, and Mia are superstars and yet still work on the basics of their sport, you've got no excuse for ignoring the basic skills of fatherhood.

4.3 GET INTO SHAPE

Recent studies have uncovered a disturbing health trend among American children: they're getting fatter. This should not surprise us, not when you consider that many kids prefer a steady diet of television, pizza, and video games to broccoli, salmon and cottage cheese.

We can't just blame our tubby kids for their condition. Who do you think is their number one role model when it comes to fitness? It isn't some TV star (they know they'll never be that skinny) or video hero (even kids know the difference between pixels and pecs). It's their dads!

And what do they see us doing? On any given weekend they see us glued to a game on television, while we hold a piece of pizza in one hand and cover the other with one of those giant foam "We're Number One" fingers. We might not be adept at playing the latest video game, but we can operate the remote with blazing dexterity.

So, if you want your kids to slim down, try a little exercise and healthy eating yourself. They will watch in wonder as you get into shape, and it won't be long before they adopt your lifestyle.

There's another benefit to getting into shape. You'll have a much greater chance of long-term survival, and we mean that literally. Not only will you get to see your kids grow into adulthood, but you'll likely be around to enjoy their kids. Now there's a health benefit!

SAFE OR DANGEROUS?

As a dad, you'll want to play games with your child. Regardless of your kid's age, safety should always be a consideration. Whether you'll be playing board games indoors or recreational sports outside, you must take into account the risk factor for each activity.

Most dads know the inherent dangers in popular sports like football, soccer, and basketball. (Baseball doesn't have any inherent dangers except for boredom.) But what about other activities? Don't be fooled. Even though these games appear to be much safer, the risk of injury is high.

As a public service, we offer the following safety analysis:

ACTIVITY	RATING	EXPLANATION
Tiddly Winks	Dangerous	A tiddly could ricochet off the wall and knock the wink out your eye
Badminton	Dangerous	You could die of asphyxiation if the shuttlecock flies into your mouth as you pant during a vigorous volley
Billiards	Dangerous	Imagine the pain if your child makes an errant shot and accidentally reams you with the cue stick
Bowling	Dangerous	This activity has all the components for disaster. A twelve-pound bowling ball and toes. Need we say more?

4.4 NURSING YOUR INJURIES

Despite the pre-game stretching and calisthenics, and even with all of the padding and special safety equipment, athletes get injured. It's not uncommon to see blood, teeth, or eyeballs left on the playing field. Fatherhood isn't any safer than most sports. Oh, sure, you aren't likely to rupture a kidney while you are helping your child with a school project, but you can sustain a different type of injury that takes just as long to heal.

The injuries that dads get are usually self-inflicted. We aren't talking about shooting your toe off while you're cleaning your shotgun. We're talking about those times when we make a colossal mess in our relationship with our kids. Maybe we lose our temper and explode in anger. Maybe we are guilty of some moral failing that was obviously wrong at the outset. A father suffers no greater pain than when he sees that he has disappointed and disillusioned his child.

So what happens when we sustain such an injury? We don't have the same type of choices that are available to injured athletes. We can't choose to take early retirement from fatherhood. We are in that game for life. Nope, the only option for us is to dedicate ourselves to a rehabilitation regimen. We might be on the disabled list for a little while, but we need to work hard to get back into the starting lineup.

INJURIES ARE INEVITABLE BUT IF YOU WORK HARD AT THE RECOVERY AND REHABILITATION, YOUR INJURY DOESN'T HAVE TO BE THE END OF YOUR CAREER AS A DAD. YOU CAN MAKE A COMEBACK.

This may require some frank

conversations with your child. Most of us guys like to brag about our victories, but we prefer to be mute when it comes to our failures. Well, the silent treatment will only prolong the recovery process and it may even aggravate the injury. If you want that injury to heal, your rehab will include confession and apology.

Injuries are inevitable (especially given the male tendency toward stupidity). But if you work hard at the recovery and rehabilitation, your injury doesn't have to be the end of your career as a dad. You can make a comeback.

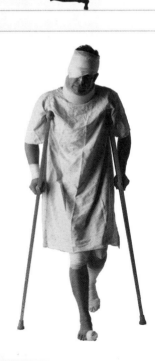

We've been making comparisons between sports and the job of being a dad. If you think we're trivializing the sacred role of fatherhood, consider this: the Bible uses a sports analogy to talk about your relationship with God:

> *All athletes practice strict self-control. They do it to win a prize that will fade away, but we do it for an eternal prize. (1 Corinthians 9:25).*

In the game of life, finishing the race means winning the race. Once you begin the process of being a dad, you've got to commit yourself to being faithful to your kids as long as you have breath left in your weary lungs. Giving up means you lose, and so do your kids. As you run (believe us, a dad is always running), remember that your influence on your kids will be huge. You may not be the Tiger Woods of dads, but you will be the biggest champion they know.

ONCE YOU BEGIN THE PROCESS OF BEING A DAD, YOU'VE GOT TO COMMIT YOURSELF TO BEING FAITHFUL TO YOUR KIDS AS LONG AS YOU HAVE BREATH LEFT IN YOUR WEARY LUNGS.

> *Remember that in a race everyone runs, but only one person gets the prize. You also must run in such a way that you will win (1 Corinthians 9:24).*

05

COMMUNICATING & CONNECTING

5.0 CAN WE TALK?

So far in this *Survival Handbook for Dads* we have explained several different types of survival techniques for dads:

Start with a plan	**Get organized**
Pay attention to growth	**Play to win**

All of these will help you survive and thrive as a dad, but take away any one of them and you probably could still make it. However, what we are about to talk about in this chapter is something every dad needs. You might be able to survive without a great plan or effective time management, but you will fail miserably if you don't learn to communicate with your kids.

It starts when they're newborns and it continues throughout their lives. Communication includes talking, of course, but that's just a small part. It's listening, too. And connecting with your child's needs, desires, and dreams, which will come to you in ways you won't expect.

All we can do is make suggestions and give you ideas. Truthfully, all we can do is talk to you. But you can do so much more with your kids, and you should. So let's get on with it. The wonderful world of communications is waiting for you.

5.1 ESTABLISHING A CONNECTION

We live in a high tech world, and communications is at the heart of it. Through the wizardry of telecommunications satellites, we can have instantaneous communication with astronauts while they orbit the earth. (So why is it often difficult to establish a simple connection on your cell phone when you are calling home from across town?) Those navigation devices they are building into some new cars can pinpoint your location within three feet. (We only wish there was a device to help us find our car keys when we're in a hurry.)

For dads, the most important aspect of communication has nothing to do with satellites, mobile phones, or navigation systems. It is a matter of connecting with your kid one to one. The father/child connection is vital to your relationship. If you aren't communicating and connecting with each other, then you are just co-occupants of the same house.

IF YOU AREN'T CONNECTING WITH YOUR CHILD, THEN IT'S YOUR OWN FAULT. BECAUSE YOU ARE THE ONE WHO IS SUPPOSED TO BE MORE MATURE, THE BURDEN IS ON YOU TO DO WHATEVER IT TAKES TO ESTABLISH THE CONNECTION.

Connecting with your kid is more than just the mutual exchange of monosyllabic grunts as you pass in the kitchen on the way to work and school. It is more than momentary physical contact when you both grab for the TV remote in the evening. You only establish a meaningful connection when your kids know that you are interested in them.

If you aren't connecting with your child, then it's your own fault. Because you are the one who is supposed to be more mature, the burden is on you to do whatever it takes to establish the connection. It may not happen quickly. Some kids are easier to connect with than others. But the effort will be worth it. Communication happens only when the connection has been established.

— 5.2 DEALING WITH STATIC —

A while back one of the major mobile phone providers ran a series of television ads that showed the comic consequences of muddled messages. The point of the marketing campaign was to convince consumers to use a wireless system free from static or electrical interference.

As a dad trying to successfully communicate with your kids, you must consider the same thing: What good is trying to communicate with your kids if something electrical interferes with the messages? Your kids are walking, talking communications devices. Their ability to sort through electronic signals and variable frequencies is nothing short of miraculous. They can listen to their MP3 player, retrieve and send emails through their computer, and talk on their cell phone—all at once.

But just try to give them one simple verbal message—"Pick up your little brother after school"—and your chances of success are pretty slim. That's because you haven't learned to interfere with their electronic devices, and you haven't learned to use static to your advantage.

Now we're not suggesting that you actually use electricity to get their attention. No, we have a very simple and practical suggestion. The way you interfere with their electronic devices is to make a habit of sitting down, looking them in the eye, smiling, and then talking very softly. Don't try to talk over the noise in their world. Simply cut through it by using that proven method: face-to-face communication. You'll be amazed how effective it is.

5.3 CHECK YOUR MESSAGES

Your life is full of messages that people send to you. Some are marked "urgent" and are delivered overnight by Federal Express. Others arrive days or weeks later via the U.S. Postal Service. Still others are left "after the beep." And don't forget about the ones that come over the Internet in the form of email. No matter how it arrives, each message delivers a piece of information that is relevant to the sender.

Your kid is sending messages to you as well. You might not realize it at first, especially if the two of you live under the same roof. (FedEx seldom delivers from the bedroom down the hall.) But just as the conventional messages you receive tell you something about the sender, the messages from your child reveal information about your kid.

Here's a little help on how do identify and interpret the messages from your child:

WHAT YOUR KID SAYS

As a general rule, the real message is just the opposite of whatever your child says. "Yeah, everything is fine" really means that your kid has a problem that he or she doesn't want to talk about. This "opposite rule" is especially true if the spoken words go something like this, "No, dad, I'm not hiding anything from you."

WHAT YOUR KID DOESN'T SAY

Often, you'll find the message in what is not spoken. For example, suppose your kid tells you, "I didn't stay out until midnight." That may be a truthful statement, but the real message is the unspoken sentence that your child is mentally reciting: "I didn't stay out until midnight because I stayed out an hour longer."

BODY LANGUAGE

Listening to what your child says, or doesn't say, won't always help you decipher the message. Sometimes you've got to use your eyes and examine your child's body language. Slumped shoulders and a dropped head usually indicate guilt, unless your child is a teenager, in which case it just indicates poor posture. For teenagers, a message of guilt can by detected when you see them walking upright with a smile on their face (often accompanied by the phrase, "No, dad, I'm not hiding anything from you").

ACTIONS

The person who coined the phrase, "actions speak louder than words," must have been a dad referring to his child. Some kids could fool an FBI polygraph expert with their responses, and they exert such physiological control that their body language is indecipherable. If your kid falls into this category, then you'll have to resort to examining their actions. Of course, you can't follow your kid around twenty-four hours a day (but a private investigator can).

Learn to read the hidden messages that your child is sending, and you might learn things that your child never intended for you to know. That's one of the best parts of being a dad.

5.4 SHUT UP AND LISTEN

With so much technology around that facilitates communication, isn't it amazing that dads have such a difficult time talking with their kids? Yet good communication is fundamental to a successful father/child relationship. You can't thrive as a dad without it. Forget thrive; you can't even survive fatherhood without it.

The key to communicating with your child is listening to your child, but don't approach your turn at listening as simply a pause between your turns at talking. Listening is your best opportunity to understand your child. Most people do not listen with the intent to understand whomever is talking; they listen with the intent to jump in with a reply as soon as possible. When they aren't talking, they are preparing to talk.

Most of us dads are pretty impressed with our own wisdom. Compared to our kids' limited experience, we think we have a lot to offer. If only our kids would realize how much they could benefit from our insight. Because we're afraid that they are being deprived of the valuable knowledge that they need, we often commandeer every conversation as opportunity to pontificate. We labor at getting our child to understand what we're trying to say. Unfortunately, this approach centers every conversation on us.

IF YOUR CHILD HAS BEEN BORED WITH YOUR CONVERSATIONS, THEN YOU'VE BEEN TALKING TOO MUCH OR LISTENING TOO LITTLE.

If you want to revolutionize your communication with your child, try to understand what your child is saying before you try to get your child to understand you. This means that you need to listen to what your child is saying from your child's perspective. As you listen, imagine yourself in your child's frame of reference. Put yourself in your kid's world as you listen.

If your child has been bored with your conversations, then you've been talking too much or listening too little. Oh, and if you think that listening is for women or people without opinions, keep in mind that your heavenly Father listens to you. And He expects you to do the same.

> *Be silent and know that I am God!*
> *(Psalm 46:10)*

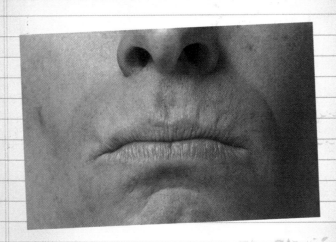

INALIENABLE WRITES

Don't expect to receive a handwritten letter from your child. It won't happen. Ever. We aren't saying that your kid won't write to you while away at summer camp or when he or she leaves home for college. Just don't expect to see your child's penmanship in any message.

These days any written communication that you'll receive from your child will most likely take the form of email. Your child's choice of email isn't based on any subconscious desire to be detached from your parentage. Email is simply the preferred technique of choice for three very practical reasons:

EFFORT

Email doesn't require the energy to address an envelope. If you expect that kind of effort from your child, you'll have to pay extra for it.

EMBARRASSMENT

Your child could be exposed to your ridicule over possible misspellings in a handwritten letter. Email has spell-check.

EXPENSE

With email, your kid won't be required to spend money on a stamp. (Instead, that money can be spent on your next Father's Day present.)

06

DUCT TAPE DAD

6.0 MR. FIX IT

As dads, we should all be thankful to Tim Allen, who starred in *Home Improvement*. In each episode, Tim "the tool man" Taylor botched a relatively simple repair job. We enjoyed that show for its humor, but we are more appreciative of the fact that it lowered our wives' expectations of our abilities to fix stuff. They still expect us to perform minor repairs, but at least they aren't surprised when we make the situation worse.

(Here is our secret: Always appear eager to undertake the repair effort, but establish a consistent record of incompetence. After a few catastrophes, your wife will know better than to ask for your help.)

YOUR KID IS GOING TO HAVE FAR FEWER BROKEN TOYS THAN DAMAGED DREAMS AND SMASHED EXPECTATIONS. SO YOU'VE GOT TO HAVE MORE IN YOUR ARSENAL THAN DUCT TAPE AND A PAIR OF VICE GRIPS. YOU'LL NEED SENSITIVITY, INSIGHT AND WISDOM.

Even if you aren't a genius with power tools, you might as well resign yourself to the fact that for some things, your middle name is "Mr. Fix It." That will be your job for as long as you are a dad. But we don't mean that you'll be expected to come to the rescue when the toilet overflows. No, your permanent role as Mr. Fix It relates to the problems that arise in the lives of your children. If something is broken or doesn't work correctly in their lives, then Dad is the go-to guy. It will be your job to remedy the situation or solve the problem.

Being Mr. Fix It is easy when the problem is nothing more than Barbie's head being snapped off; all it takes is a little glue for you to be the hero. (Please realize that we are talking about a doll. The preceding sentence should be disregarded if you have a daughter named Barbie.) For these types of situations, our advice is simple: If it can't be fixed with super glue or duct tape, then buy a new one.

Our advice gets a bit more complicated for fixing problems that involve relationships, character, or emotions. Let's face it, as dads we are more comfortable fixing a broken wagon than repairing hurt feelings. But in the course of your life as a dad, your kid is going to have far fewer broken toys than damaged dreams  and smashed expectations. So you've got to have more in your arsenal than duct tape and a pair of vice grips. You'll need sensitivity, insight and wisdom. You'll be dealing with despair and disappointment. You will be the one who must reassemble the pieces of your child's life.

All of a sudden, unplugging the toilet doesn't sound so difficult, does it?

6.1 MENDING THE BROKEN PLACES

For some dads, fixing stuff comes naturally. Maybe you are one of those guys who has an instinct for home repair. When you see (or hear) a leaky faucet, you immediately know what to do. When your lawn mower starts blowing out blue smoke, you can identify the problem. When your wife needs a new shelf in the laundry room, you spring into action, anxious to use your combination power saw/power drill/power sander/hangnail remover.

We envy guys like this, because we are among the group of dads who think they can fix stuff (what guy doesn't?), but in reality lack the skills required for everyday home maintenance (such as changing light bulbs). Oh, we enjoy roaming the aisles at Home Depot as much as the next guy, but we lack the actual ability to accomplish the desired results. Most of the time we need the help of experts (such as our sons).

There's another category of home repair that has nothing to do with hardware. It's more like dealing with software, and we don't mean computers. No, we're talking about your kids. More often than you realize, your kids need mending, and it's more than broken bones, sprained fingers or scraped knees. The emotional part of your kids requires the most attention, and very often dad is whom they need the most.

You might think you have the ability to deal with your children's emotional needs, but you have to offer more encouragement than simply saying to your sobbing daughter: "Hey, quit being such a crybaby. Take it like a man!" Just like some guys need outside help when it comes to fixing basic household problems, you might need some expert advice when it comes to mending the broken places in your child's life.

Think about it. You have a hard enough time handling your own disappointment, rejection, and failure. What are you going to do when your daughter comes to you with tears in her eyes and sputters, "Daddy, I feel so bad."

First of all, be thankful that she is coming to you. Whether she feels bad about the harsh words of a friend in kindergarten, or her heart has been broken by her first boyfriend, thank God that she trusts you enough to sob on your shoulder.

JUST LIKE SOME GUYS NEED OUTSIDE HELP WHEN IT COMES TO FIXING BASIC HOUSEHOLD PROBLEMS, YOU MIGHT NEED SOME EXPERT ADVICE WHEN IT COMES TO MENDING THE BROKEN PLACES IN YOUR CHILD'S LIFE.

What do you do next? The first part is easy. Give her your shoulder. Let her cry. Resist the urge to give her your pearls of wisdom. Instead, just listen, comfort, and hug. Then, rely on outside experts—your wife, your pastor, a helpful book on the subject—to guide you through the issue. You won't know everything there is to know (no one expects you to), but you can know something, even if it doesn't seem like much to you. That's okay, because your support will seem like everything to her.

Something in the genetic composition of every male makes him resistant to asking for help. This is not a bad thing. After all, thanks to this streak of self-reliance:

> You've explored many streets that you never would have known about if you had asked for directions and driven only on the correct route.

> You've discovered an interesting array of food products while wandering the wrong aisles in the supermarket.

> You've measured the limits of your pain threshold by walking around for three weeks with an injured groin. An individual with less personal fortitude would have wasted time and money by consulting a physician.

Self-reliance is fine when only your image is at stake. But when your kid is involved, you need to deflate your ego for the sake of your child's well being. There will be times when your kid needs help that you can't provide. Don't jeopardize their shot at success simply because you are too proud to ask for help.

Call in an expert when you can't provide the help that your child needs:

> If your daughter wants to try out for the 4th grade volleyball team but you don't know the difference between a spike and a dig, then hire a kid on the high school volleyball team

to give coaching lessons to your daughter. It may cost you $10/hour, but that is better than exposing your ignorance to your daughter.

Suppose your son needs help with his math homework. It is safe to make an attempt on your own only if the calculator he is using is in the shape of a Disney character. But if it's one of those graphing calculators with a display screen the size of a small TV monitor, then hire a math tutor.

Does your teenager have a tattoo anywhere above the neck complimented by a pierced eyelid and smoldering hair follicles? Do the shock waves of music blaring from your kid's stereo speakers loosen the shingles on your roof? Enlist a cross-cultural interpreter to help you communicate with your teenager.

Are there fist-shaped holes in your kid's bedroom walls? Is a criminal defense lawyer on your kid's AOL buddy list? Don't go into your kid's bedroom without first calling for back up.

You aren't an expert in everything. If your child is involved in the areas where you are lacking in knowledge or ability, be quick to get outside help. If you need to know what those areas are, just ask your mother-in-law. She has already made a long list.

PLUGGING THE LEAKS

Kids cry. It's what they do. We aren't just talking about infants (although it seems that they spend a disproportionate amount of their waking hours engaged in this activity). Whatever the age of your child, you better expect some tears. As the dad, you'll be expected to offer words of comfort and "make things better."

There are two guidelines that you must follow if you are going to respond properly to a crying child.

AGE	HYPOTHETICAL SITUATION	YOUR RESPONSE
1-5	Your toddler cries when he bangs his noggin on the corner of the coffee table.	Grab a dishtowel. It can be used to muffle the shrieking. Later, it can be used for wiping the blood off the corner of the table.
6-10	You first-grader sobs when she falls into a mud puddle on the playground.	You can't comfort her over the phone. You'll have to go to school to bring her a clean change of clothes. Console her, but don't let the little urchin get mud on the leather seats of your car.
11-15	Your 12-year old son cries when he gets cut from the basketball team.	Most dads make the rookie mistake of saying something insensitive like, "Stop crying. Men don't cry." We suggest that you let your son cry his eyes out. Then say, "Maybe you are better suited for a sissy sport, like shuffleboard."
16-20	Your daughter whimpers after flunking her driver's license exam.	First, check the car to make sure she didn't flunk by crunching a fender. Then tell her that you'll be available to drive her to all of her social events for the rest of high school. (That will give her a real reason to cry.)

1. Display tough love. You don't want to be considered as thoughtless and tactless, but you don't want to coddle or cater to your crying child.

2. Take it to the next level. You must modify and adapt your consoling techniques as your child grows older.

Here are examples of some of the techniques that you may wish to employ:

AGE	HYPOTHETICAL SITUATION	YOUR RESPONSE
21-25	Your son gets teary-eyed at his graduation from college.	Do nothing. He's only mourning the fact that financial support from you is coming to a screeching halt.
26-30	Your daughter cries at her wedding.	You'll score extra points if you cry too in a display of emotional empathy. Your tears should come naturally, but if you have difficulty, then take these two steps: First, remind yourself that you are losing your little princess to some unworthy buffoon. Secondly, calculate how much the wedding is costing you.
Over 30	Your son cries when his daughter gets cut from the soccer team.	Don't feel sorry for him. He isn't thinking about your granddaughter's feelings. He is only thinking about himself. He's fearful that she'll miss the opportunity for an athletic scholarship that could save him big bucks in tuition payments. Slap him on the side of his head and tell him, "Stop being a baby. Men don't cry."

6.3 DAMAGE CONTROL

Every once in a while something very big is going to happen to your family. This won't be "win the lottery" big (this only happens to unemployed dock workers or Starbuck's employees). And it probably won't be "lost your home in a hurricane" big (this only happens to residents in South Florida in odd numbered leap years). No, the kind of "big" we're referring to are the ordinary opportunities and challenges that all families encounter. Here are some examples:

> You get an offer for the dream job of a lifetime, but it requires you to uproot your family from their friends, schools and favorite shopping mall, and move them to a city with an uninhabitable climate, restaurants that cook with lard, and an annual Flannel Festival.

> You think your son is doing well in school, but one day the principal calls and informs you that not only is your son failing the third grade, but he has been extorting milk money from younger kids in exchange for "protection."

> Your brother-in-law's "can't miss" investment strategy turns into a sure-fire disaster, preventing you from taking your wife on that anniversary cruise you've been promising.

Every family is going to go through times of unusual opportunity and incredible challenge, so don't panic when these things happen. Instead of covering up and placing blame like politicians do, we recommend this strategy:

Don't deny the problem, admit it. 'Fess up rather than cover up. However, don't use the truth like a hammer. Be aware of your family's feelings.

Instead of plugging the leaks, fix the source. Duct tape has many amazing uses, but fixing leaks is not one of them. You can't patch the problem where it's spurting out. You've got to go to the source and correct the wrong.

Instead of moving on as if nothing happened, learn from your mistakes. It doesn't do any good to admit the problem and fix the source unless you learn from the mistakes you made.

EVERY FAMILY IS GOING TO GO THROUGH TIMES OF UNUSUAL OPPORTUNITY AND INCREDIBLE CHALLENGE, SO DON'T PANIC WHEN THESE THINGS HAPPEN.

These basic survival techniques aren't terribly detailed, but they are enough to get you on the right track. You can't ask any more than that (and neither can your family).

Put down the plunger. Set the sockets aside. Hang the hammer back on the pegboard. None of your favorite tools is going help when you are trying to fix the problems in your child's life.

Just as every man needs at least a few basic fix-it tools, every dad needs to have at least five skills honed and ready to employ when his kid is going through difficult times.

HUMOR

Don't overlook the importance of this skill. The crying will stop if you can get the laughter started. If your kid isn't at a point of being able to laugh at himself, then turn his attention to the many things about you that are laughable. (You'll never run out of examples.)

ENCOURAGEMENT

The first rule of repair is to hit the thing that isn't working. This rule applies to televisions, toasters and transmissions; it isn't usually the best approach with children. Oh, sure, a slap on the buttocks may be helpful on a few occasions, but a preferred approach is a pat on the back. The distance between those two parts of your child's anatomy is only a few vertebrae, so make sure you aim high.

SARCASM

Just as a novice woodworker shouldn't use a lathe, you shouldn't attempt to use sarcasm unless you're

experienced with it. Used improperly, it can cause
serious damage. But if you can use it properly, in
the right circumstance it might give your child the
motivational incentive that is needed for the moment.

SYMPATHY

Women use their shoulders as a place for hanging
their purse strap. As a dad, use yours for your
child. Every kid needs a dad's shoulder to cry on.
(Note: If you are carrying a purse, that may be the
reason your kid is crying.)

ATTENTION

Many of the problems in your child's life can be
solved, or at least minimized, if you pay attention
to your child. Your kid needs to talk with someone
about the rough spots in life. That someone can be
you, or the school psychologist, or some predator in
a chat room. When you look at those options, suddenly
you become the best choice. Way to go, dad.

6.5 MAKE SURE THE FOUNDATION IS RIGHT

In this chapter we've pretty much focused on fixing things, and that's good. When problems arise, you've got to know how to get things back to the way they were, and sometimes make them even better. But life is more than just making repairs. It's also about doing things right in the first place so you don't have to constantly solve problems and correct mistakes.

Take your house. You could design an impressive exterior and decorate the inside in the most beautiful way possible, but it would all crumble and crack if the foundation wasn't solid. You can't see the foundation, but it's the most important ingredient. It's where you start.

The same thing goes for your family. As a dad, your primary task is to make sure the foundation is solid. If there are weaknesses, or the base isn't true, then you are going to be spending your life fixing and repairing rather than building and improving. That's not to say that troubles and problems won't come. They will, both for you and your kids. But you'll be able to weather the storms a lot better if your foundation is built on the right stuff.

> Though the rain comes in torrents and the floodwaters rise and the winds beat against that house, it won't collapse, because it is build on rock (Matthew 7:25).

90

WHAT ARE YOU, MADE OF MONEY?

7.0 THE MIDDLE OF MONEY

There's a famous verse in the Bible that goes something like this: "Money is the root of all evil." At least that's what people think it says, so they end up ignoring the verse (unless they don't have any money, in which case they quote it in a very pious manner), or they decide to quit reading the Bible so they won't feel guilty about making money.

Actually, there's no such verse in the Bible, so you can rest assured that God doesn't hate money. That's not to say that God doesn't have an opinion about money. Here's what the verse really says:

> *For the love of money is at the root of all kinds of evil (1 Timothy 6:10).*

Notice that it's not money itself that's evil, but the love of money. And even that's not evil, but it's at the root—or the cause—of all kinds of evil.

OTHER THINGS THE BIBLE DOES NOT SAY ABOUT MONEY

God helps those who help themselves.

A penny saved is a penny earned.

In God we trust—all others pay cash.

Whatever you want to call it—greed, selfishness, keeping up with the Joneses—loving money leads to no good. On the other hand, hating money also leads to no good. The trick is to be somewhere in the middle, which is where we're going to be in this chapter.

We aren't going to offer any advice on how to increase your financial standing (if we had some good tips, we'd be using them ourselves), and we won't steer you down a dead end money trail (we've already been there, and it's not a pretty sight). Instead, we will do our best to help you and your kids develop healthy and realistic attitudes toward money.

You don't need to be a money maven to know that kids are costly. Even new dads expect kid-related expenditures for food, clothing and housing. But there are hidden expenses that you might not anticipate. We consider it our job—being in the brotherhood of fatherhood—to warn you about these concealed costs. We'll start with the three "C's" of unexpected expenses:

CULTURE

Moms want their children to be cultured, whereas dads are proud if their kids can burp the alphabet. In pursuit of culture, your child will receive massive maternal influence to take lessons on some sort of musical instrument. This means that you will need to budget for buying an instrument. Don't make the mistake of encouraging a small instrument just because it appears cheaper; we recommend that you insist that your child take piano lessons. Why? Well, a piano costs more initially, but your child will never lose a piano, so you'll only have to buy one of them.

COMMUNICATION

The unexpected costs of communication don't begin until your child reaches the teen years. Until that time, there is a constant flow of verbiage from your child, often at dinnertime and always during your favorite television show. Once your child becomes a teenager, however, if you want to keep the lines of communication open, you'll need to factor in the cost of a mobile phone and a family therapist.

COUNTENANCE

We aren't referring to your child's appearance, because you already know that you'll be financially responsible for your kid's contact lenses, braces and acne medication. The hidden, unexpected costs of child rearing include the expenditures for *your* appearance. To your surprise, you will find that you age exponentially faster than your child, but you will want to maintain the deception that you are young, virile, and fit. This is an admirable subterfuge, but a costly one. You'll need to budget for Rogaine (or at least Grecian Formula). And don't forget about the cost of a membership at the gym. (Your other dadly responsibilities will make you too tired to work out regularly, but you'll walk more studly just knowing that you have the membership.)

Maybe you are thinking that the costs associated with these three "C's" aren't too exorbitant. You're right, and that's the good news. The bad news is that there are three more unexpected expenses for every other letter of the alphabet.

It starts when they are very young, often before they can talk. Your kids use hand gestures, grunts, and intense body language when they hear a dilapidated ice cream truck three blocks away. They frantically seek your attention for a single purpose: to extract money from your pocket so they can buy an artificial frozen substance on a stick.

That's when it starts, but that's not where it ends. Giving your toddler money for the first time is like opening Pandora's Box, only in your case the "box" is your wallet, and the stuff that comes out is your money. And once you open it, it's impossible to close—ever! From ice cream the requests will progress to action figures, video games, name brand jeans, and car insurance. The only thing you can hope to do is control the flow of cash so you can hang on to a portion of your income in order to afford your own small luxuries, such as groceries, the mortgage, and underwear.

The key to cash flow is knowing when to say yes and when to say no to the millions of requests you will receive from your children. That's why we want to offer these tips on what to do when your kids ask for money.

If the money is for junk food—even ice cream—never hold back. Every body needs (iced) milk and besides, it might fill up your child, preventing him or her from eating more expensive food items, such as vegetables, grains, and meat.

If the money is for video games or computer software, be discerning. Shell out only for those games you would enjoy playing, such as a fantasy football game. Resist the urge to pay for so-called educational games because your kids may learn something, which would undermine your theory that all non-sports video games are evil.

On the subject of cars, gas, and insurance, the best tactic is to discourage your child from wanting to drive in the first place. Explain the inherent dangers of an automobile (especially if it is a 1991 Hyundai Scoupe), the environmental hazards of unleaded gasoline, and the blackmail tactics of insurance companies. (No father in history has been able to successfully deter his child from wanting a car, so if you succeed in being the first, please let us know.)

We haven't even touched on the most cash-draining expense category of all, and that's college. We don't mean to frighten you, but the costs of a college education will make anything else you have paid for seem like an ice cream sandwich. Your kids will be aware of the financial hardship you are under, so while they are in college you can expect them to ask for money using hand gestures, grunts, and intense body language.

SAVING ENOUGH FOR COLLEGE

(IT'S POSSIBLE, BUT THEN SO IS WINNING THE LOTTERY)

One of the major responsibilities of a dad is to save enough money so his kids can go to college. This can be an unsettling experience for a dad, because he never really knows if his nest egg will be enough, at least not until his precious little baby starts that

AMOUNT SAVED	IVY LEAGUE SCHOOL
$50 month	Residence Hall parking pass for one semester
$100 month	Parking, science books (used) and computer cable modem service for one semester
$250 month	Parking, books, cable modem, and tuition for a 2 unit Intro to Psych class taught by a T.A.
$500 month	Parking, the books, cable, the Psych class, and your choice of one of three class rings
$1000 month plus the mortgage to your home and your IRA	You might be able to get your kid through four years as long as you qualify as a hardship case and get financial aid

first semester at the University of Southern North Dakota (at Fargo).

In order to help you get a better perspective on your monthly college savings plan, here is a chart showing just how far your educational dollar will go on today's Ivy League school, state university, and community college campus. The dollars represent the amount saved per month, per kid, beginning five minutes after birth.

STATE UNIVERSITY	COMMUNITY COLLEGE
Room & Board for one year	Tuition, books, and fees for two years
Room & Board plus gas and snack food money for one year	Books, tuition, fees, and a down payment on a three-bedroom condo that can be rented to state university students
Room & Board, gas and snack food, plus tuition for 8 units (books optional)	Everything related to education, the condo, and enough to pay for the new automotive arts building
A complete college education and all the snack food your kid can possibly eat	This will educate your kid plus 12 foreign exchange students
If you can save this much money, you may as well set your kid up in business rather than pay for his or her education.	Start your own community college

7.3 A PENNY SAVED IS JUST A PENNY

Let the Federal Reserve Board worry about the national debt; your major concern must be your own bank account. As a dad you will walk a financial tight rope. As long as you have kids living at home, you might as well resign yourself to being broke, but with a little planning, you might be able to stay out of debt. It won't be easy, but here are five ways that you can save:

EATING AT HOME

Forget giving your children a variety of vittles. Forget the four basic food groups. You can save lots of money on your food bill if you simply tell your kids that there are two mealtime choices: take it or leave it.

DINING OUT

This is an expensive venture; you reserve it as a rare treat. Use it sparingly as a way to celebrate some occasion in your child's life, such as a birthday, graduation, or when your child performed well at a sporting event (and, more importantly, when they didn't do so well). To show your generosity, let your child select the dining establishment, but limit your child's choices to one of two categories: (1) Any place where the food is served on a plastic tray; or (2) Any one of those wholesale clubs where they offer free samples in the food section.

BABYSITTERS

A babysitter is just a teenager who takes money from you for teaching things to your young, impressionable children that you don't want them to learn until they are older. Don't waste your money. Use a grandmother instead. You won't have to pay her, and she might actually watch your children, whereas a babysitter is more inclined to watch your television. If there is no grandmother in the vicinity, just drop your kids off at a nearby nursing home. Eighty percent of the residents there will answer to the name "Grandma."

CHRISTMAS

Join a "Christmas Savings Club" at your bank. This will force you to put away a little money every week. Start in January, and by November you might have enough to payoff your credit card charges for last year's gifts.

SELF-IMPOSED MONETARY RESTRAINTS

If you are thinking about a budget, forget about it. Children make it impossible to stay within a budget. A better alternative is to move to a neighborhood where there are lower economic expectations and the children aren't interested in the latest fashion trends or the newest video technology. We suggest any Amish community.

7.4 WHEN BLOWING YOUR
DOLLARS MAKES SENSE

We've been talking a lot about controlling expenses and watching your cash flow, which is fine for guys like us who are a little loose with the buck. But what if you're the kind of guy who has just the opposite tendency? If we looked up the word "tightwad" in the dictionary, would we see your picture next to the definition? Do you still have the first dollar you ever made—from that grade school lemonade stand?

If you need to loosen your money belt a little, then you've come to the right place. We have plenty of experience when it comes to spending too much and saving too little, and we can tell you that sometimes it makes perfect sense.

For example, when was the last time you announced to your kids, "We're going to Disney World" (or Disneyland, or Cedar Point or Six Flags)? At least one time in your life you need to do the unexpected and unreasonable and blow a weekend and a bunch of money at a theme park. Your kids will love it and never forget the experience.

AT LEAST ONE TIME IN YOUR LIFE YOU NEED TO DO THE UNEXPECTED AND UNREASONABLE AND BLOW A WEEKEND AND A BUNCH OF MONEY AT A THEME PARK. YOUR KIDS WILL LOVE IT AND NEVER FORGET THE EXPERIENCE.

Have you ever gone way over your head by putting in a pool or buying a ski boat? We have, and we can say that although it's a strain at first, such an investment pays huge dividends down the road.

You can blow your dollars on little stuff as well as big. When is the last time you took the family out for dinner and a movie. We're talking about a real dinner (not Jack in the Box) and a prime time movie (not a matinee). Or what about one of those concerts your kids would love to see? Yes, there are some unsuitable shows and environments, but there are plenty of good ones. Hey, you can even drive your kids and sit in the back of the arena (while they sit near the front, of course).

And then there are those "priceless" outings that don't cost a dime, except for your time and a little gas: a day in the mountains, an afternoon at the beach, a trip to the zoo. Your kids love this stuff, and often what they love most is that they get to spend time with you.

One of the most daunting challenges for any dad is to maintain a proper perspective toward money. Unless you are careful, you'll have an improper attitude about money, mainly because you won't have much of it for the first twenty to thirty years of fatherhood. You'll feel like an automatic teller machine as your kids keep pulling cash out of you. No matter how hard you work, no matter how much you earn, it will never seem like enough. When you look at your paltry bank balance, you are likely to be disappointed and discouraged. Don't be. Change your perspective. Raise your sights. Take your eyes off that minuscule balance on your statement and start looking at your children. They are the reason you work so hard.

Instead of looking at money as your source of security and a measure of your success, consider it as the means of providing for your children and giving them a foundation upon which they can build a successful life. With each child, you've got about twenty years or so of financial responsibility. That responsibility applies not only to what you buy for them with your money, but also to what you teach them about money. You won't be doing them any favors if you give them lots of stuff but deprive them of the knowledge of what is really valuable in life.

Of course, if you want to teach your children a proper perspective about money, you must reflect it in your own life. That means that you can't get so wrapped up in your quest to possess that your kid feels like a fatherless child. And it means that your conduct and conversations must reinforce principles such as:

The value of a person is not determined by his or her net worth.

Friendships are more important than financial statements.

Contentment is never achieved through acquisitions.

Everyone is looking for an investment that returns a high rate of interest. You can stop looking because, as a dad, your best investment involves your children. Invest your interest in the things that matter most in life. Money isn't even on the list, but your kids are near the top of it. Always remember that finances have nothing to do with the value of your relationship with your child.

ALWAYS REMEMBER THAT FINANCES HAVE NOTHING TO DO WITH THE VALUE OF YOUR RELATIONSHIP WITH YOUR CHILD.

Don't store up treasures here on earth, where they can be eaten by moths and get rusty, and where thieves break in and steal. Store your treasures in heaven, where they will never become moth-eaten or rusty and where they will be safe from thieves. Wherever your treasure is, there your heart and thoughts will be also (Matthew 6:19-21).

08

FAMILY AND FRIENDS

8.0 ONE IS THE LONELIEST NUMBER

Way back in the beginning, there was only one guy, and his name was Adam (true story). On certain days—when life is crowding you out and the decibel level in your house exceeds the noise on an airport runway—you might envy Adam in his solitary state. There he was in this perfect garden with plenty of food and every kind of animal around him, and the fishing must have been perfect. It was paradise! There was only one problem: Adam was lonely.

God recognized this.

> *"It is not good for the man to be alone,"* *said God. "I will make a companion who will* *help him"* (Genesis 2:18).

Adam went from being a lonely guy to having a wife and kids, and that's the way it's been ever since. Man gets lonely, man gets married, and man and wife have kids.

Ever since that day guys with families have not been lonely. They have been frustrated, henpecked, harassed, and broke, but they haven't been lonely. When you think about it, that's a pretty good trade-off. A man can overcome frustration and financial ruin, but he can't do much about loneliness all by himself.

If families are a gift from God, so are friendships. The way we see it, friends are no substitute for families, but they can be just as important. The Bible says:

> *"A real friend sticks closer than a brother"*

(Proverbs 18:24).

The antidote to loneliness—and the key to fulfillment—is to keep your friends close, and your family even closer. You may think you could make it solo sometimes, but that's no way to live.

> *"God places the lonely in families"*
> *(Psalm 68:6)*

and He gives us friends to help us in times of need.

You want to teach your children necessary and important skills they will need in order to survive in adulthood. So you devote significant time to teaching the techniques of throwing a ball, riding a bike, and driving a car. That's great, but many adults don't spend much time driving (because they take mass transit), or biking (except the environmentally sensitive citizens of Oregon), and they hardly ever throw a ball (unless their occupation is juggling or baseball). The odds are much greater that your child will end up being married than throwing a ball for a living, so don't forget to show your child what it takes to make a good marriage.

For most men, marriage is like eating horseradish. They say they like it, but it brings tears to their eyes. It may be harmless fun to joke about marriage when you are hanging out with the guys, but showing disrespect for marriage in front of your children will undermine their future marital stability. No matter how funny you think it is, stay away from comments to your children that go something like this:

> "Son, to have a good marriage, you've got to find a rich wife who is too proud to have her husband work."

> "The best way to save your marriage from divorce is to stay away from the wedding."

> "Kids, I've stayed married to your mom because on Valentine's Day I always remember

to send flowers to the woman I love. And that reminds me to send a bouquet to your mom, too."

We are all for humor in the family, but your children should be convinced that you are seriously in love with your wife. Your commitment and respect for her should be the standard that your children use when they are deciding about marriage.

Surveys reveal that most girls marry men like their fathers. That may explain why at most weddings the mother of the bride is always crying. Your marriage is going to influence your child's marriage—for good or for bad. If you want to help your child have a successful marriage, then love your wife (and let your kid know it).

It's one thing to love your family, and another thing entirely to love being with them. You've met the dad who tells you how devoted he is to his family. He's got photos of the wife and kids all over his office, and he brags about their accomplishments. But there's something hollow about his words, because on weekends he plays golf or "catches up" at the office.

Then there's the guy who refers to his wife as the "old ball and chain" and who admits that his kids drive him nuts sometimes. Basically he likes having a family, but he'd rather do something with his buddies than do nothing with his family.

We're confident that we're not describing you—if we were, you wouldn't be reading this book. You recognize that no family is perfect, but you realize that you have a responsibility to care for, protect and love those precious people God has entrusted to you. They're not a burden to you; they are a blessing.

Dads who remain loyal to their own selfish ideas of manhood are chauvinists. Dads who treat their families with honor and respect are chivalrous. The words may sound alike, but the men they describe are worlds apart. Why not bring back the age-old practice of chivalry in your household. You don't have to dress up like a knight (unless your wife finds it unusually attractive) but you can be just as noble (which she will find even more attractive).

— 8.3 LOVE 'EM AND LEAVE 'EM —

The great thing about your extended family is that you don't have to see them very often, and when you do, it's usually at a time and a place with plenty of distractions and alternate activities. These would include wedding receptions, Christmas dinners, bar mitzvahs, and Fourth of July picnics.

The real challenge comes every few years when you drag the wife and kids (or your wife drags you) to a family reunion. These elaborate affairs usually last for a weekend, which is just enough time for other families to get on your family's nerves. Actually, this is why family reunions are a healthy thing. Before you go, you may think your own family is a little unusual. Then you spend forty-eight hours with your siblings and cousins and aunts and uncles and their strange broods, and you begin to appreciate your own family dynamics.

By the end of the reunion, you all breathe a collective sigh of relief. You love your extended family, but it feels good to leave them. You thank God for your wonderful wife and kids and say aloud, "Aren't we glad we're not like they are." Of course, what you don't realize is that every other family is saying the same thing about you.

8.4 MAKE FRIENDS

BECAUSE YOU'LL NEED THEM

Friends are actually better than relatives. The relationship can be just as close as family ties, but you get to choose your friends. Take advantage of that opportunity. Choose a few select friends now, because you are sure to need them later.

Let's face facts. As a dad, you are going to need all of the help that you can get. This book can only do so much for you. After the last page, you'll be on your own. But it doesn't have to be that way. A few strategically developed friendships can give you the guidance, encouragement and accountability that you need to keep you on track for being a great dad.

Obtaining friends is not the problem. Friends are easy to find, especially if you are generous. But friends that you can buy aren't worth the price that you pay for them. The trick is to find true friends who are willing to put more into the friendship than they want to get out of it. In other words, they are willing to help you be a better dad because they care about you and your kid. Here's some of the criteria that you should be looking for in a true friend:

He'll listen to you explain the struggles you are having with your kid and will feel that they are his problems too (even if he doesn't have kids);

He will pull you up when you are down, but he will also bring you down when you are too puffed up;

When you blow it as a dad, he'll remind you that the damage isn't permanent;

He'll be brave enough to say your faults to your face, but he'll never be a weasel and say those things behind your back;

He'll stay your friend even when he gets to know you real well.

THE BENEFIT OF HAVING TRUE FRIENDS IS THAT THEY CAN HELP YOU BECOME A BETTER PERSON. WHEN YOU BECOME A BETTER PERSON, YOU BECOME A BETTER DAD.

The benefit of having true friends is that they can help you become a better person. When you become a better person, you become a better dad. Of course, this means that you'll need to find friends who inspire you to improve. These will need to be guys who have character qualities that are superior to yours. It shouldn't be hard to find guys like this. Just ask your wife. Shortly before you were married, her mother gave her a long list of such candidates in an attempt to sabotage your engagement. Your wife probably doesn't have the list any more, but we're sure that your mother-in-law made copies.

→

8.5 THE VILLAGE PEOPLE

According to an old saying, it takes a village to raise a child. When you first consider this statement, it seems to be partially correct, but also partially wrong:

> Partially Correct: Raising a child requires more than you have to offer. Hey, you are just one man. Your child needs a woman's influence. Your kid needs the affection and guidance of grandparents. Extended family and friends are also a valuable and necessary component in your child's life. In other words, raising a child is more than a one-man job.

> Partially Wrong: But the whole village doesn't need to be involved in the process of raising your child. In fact, there are lots of people in the village that you might want to exclude as influences in your child's life. We don't need to elaborate— you know who these village idiots are.

On further reflection, however, imagine if your child's "village" could be comprised solely of the family members and friends who have your child's best interest at heart. If the village is defined and populated in that fashion, then, yes, it does take the entire village to raise a child.

At the risk of straining the analogy a little further, we want to challenge you to assume the role of immigration officer of your child's village. In other words, as the dad, you should take the initiative to determine who belongs in the village. You are the guard at the gate. You need to make sure that your kid is surrounded by positive influences and protected from people who could be detrimental to your child.

YOU CAN'T RAISE YOUR CHILD ALONE. YOU ARE GOING TO NEED HELP. BUT YOU GET TO DECIDE WHO IS GOING TO JOIN YOU IN THE PROCESS.

This is a job that requires some skill. Your young child will enjoy having a protector, but your teenager is more apt to view you as a warden. And this is not a part-time job. You must be on the alert at all time, or at least while your child is awake (which during infancy and the teen years may seem like all of the time).

You can't raise your child alone. You are going to need help. But you get to decide who is going to join you in the process. Don't settle for inferior assistants. The welfare of your child depends upon whom you allow into the village.

> *Tune your ears to wisdom, and concentrate on understanding. Cry out for insight and understanding. Search for them as you would for lost money or hidden treasure. Then you will understand what it means to fear the Lord, and you will gain knowledge of God. For the Lord grants wisdom!...*
>
> *He grants a treasure of good sense to the godly. He is their shield, protecting those who walk with integrity (Proverbs 2:2-7).*

09

PROCEED WITH CAUTION

Most dads aren't schizophrenic, but they are living in two worlds. There's the world as it really is, and then there is the world as they want it to be. It is our guess that you are the same as most dads, so your two worlds look like this:

IN THE REAL WORLD

You aren't perfect. You make mistakes. Lots of them. And a few of them are real whoppers (and we aren't talking about burgers).

IN THE WORLD AS YOU WANT IT TO BE

Your kid doesn't know about your mistakes. Your child thinks you are perfect. (Your wife knows better, but she is kind enough not to spoil your child's delusion of your perfection.)

When we refer to mistakes that you want to conceal from your kids, we aren't talking about the minor and often humorous flubs like burning the toast, spilling the juice, or dropping the baby on its head. We are referring to those more embarrassing and discrediting flaws in your personality, like losing your temper (with the associated expletives and gestures) or making bad choices that have detrimental consequences.

Don't delude yourself. You child is well aware of your failings. If your kid is an infant, then most of your blunders have no present consequence, but the image of them has been imbedded in your child's subconscious for future reference. If your children are teenagers, now is the time of future reference. Your kids can't remember to call home if they are going to be late, but somehow they remember your screw-ups from the prior decade. As to your current mistakes, there is no time delay—your kids will point them out as soon as you commit them.

We don't presume to have the knowledge or ability that would be required to keep you from committing future mistakes. (That is a fantasy world where only your wife lives.) Our humble task in this chapter is to merely assist you on the road to recovery after you have blown it. You don't need to thank us. We know you'll do the same thing for another dad if you have the chance. And given the frequency with which dads make mistakes, you ought to have lots of chances.

Do you think you're a pretty good dad? We hope so. Every father needs to know how important he is to the family he helped start. We hope your kids have given you one of those cheesy "World's Greatest Dad" miniature trophies, or a two-sizes-too-small "No. 1 Dad" T-shirt. You need to believe that your family looks up to you and counts on you to be their leader and example.

Having said that, we want to remind you that you're not perfect—none of us are, not even those TV dads from the 1950s. We all make mistakes as dads because we're all human. The thing is, you don't want to hide behind your excuses and perpetuate the myth of perfection, because your kids know better. You don't want to adopt a "Do as I do, not as I say" philosophy, because your kids can see right through it (even worse, they'll eventually copy your behavior).

So what do you do when you fall off the pedestal of perfection? How do you handle it when you're not worthy of wearing the "No. 1 Dad" shirt? We don't mean to get overly philosophical or spiritual here, but we have learned a few things about failure, and we thought we'd share our experiences with you.

First of all, admit you're not perfect. That shouldn't be too hard, although it might be difficult to admit it to your family. Second, when you do something wrong, ask forgiveness—first from God, then from your wife, and finally from your kids. You don't need to go into great detail with your kids. Just be honest and tell them you blew it. Leaders become leaders because of their integrity, and integrity starts with honesty.

Integrity also means that you're the same person in private as you are in public. The dad your kids see at home should be the same guy they don't see at the office or on a business trip.

> **WHEN YOU DO SOMETHING WRONG, ASK FORGIVENESS—FIRST FROM GOD, THEN FROM YOUR WIFE, AND FINALLY FROM YOUR KIDS. . . . JUST BE HONEST AND TELL THEM YOU BLEW IT.**

Finally, realize that God loves you despite your faults. (Isn't that Good News?) He wants you to lead your family, and He promises to help you earn the right—if you ask Him. You may have been given the title of "dad" when you had your first child, but it's a title you need to earn every day. And that includes earning the right to get back on the pedestal when you fall off.

If you are susceptible to a guilty conscience, then we suggest that you refrain from listening to the radio for the week preceding Father's Day each June. During that week, virtually every radio station on the planet plays that "Cat's In the Cradle" song by Harry Chapin.

This song tells the story of a dad who was too busy to play with his son during every stage of childhood. When the dad is old and retired, he finally wants to spend time with his son, but by that time the son is too preoccupied to be interested in his father. It is the "like father, like son" story that challenges every dad make time for the most important thing: his child.

We know your excuses (because we have used them ourselves):

> "I'm swamped at work. I'll spend extra time with the kids as soon as this project is finished."

> "I've been working hard all week, and I'm exhausted. If I don't get some rest, then I won't be any good to anybody."

> "I have to have some time to wind down. I'll be more fun to be with if I get in a little recreation for myself. The kids won't turn into juvenile delinquents while I play just one round of golf."

You probably have a few personal favorites you can add to the list. Let's face it, you can always come up with an excuse if you are weak enough to use one. But don't. Decide right now that your time is not your own as long as you have kids at home. Spend as much time with them as you can. Treat them as a priority in your life. If you don't, you're going to blow it as a dad.

We know you have a busy schedule (that is part of the definition of fatherhood.) But if Tiger Woods asked you to drive him around in a golf cart at Pebble Beach, you would find the time. And we are sure that you'd throw your PDA out the window if Michelle Pfeiffer asked you to be a production assistant on her next movie.

DECIDE RIGHT NOW THAT YOUR TIME IS NOT YOUR OWN AS LONG AS YOU HAVE KIDS AT HOME.

These are people you don't even know, and they aren't interested in knowing you (especially Michelle). But if you could make time for them, you should be able to carve out some time for your child—whom you do know (hopefully) and who is interested in knowing you (hopefully). If you don't know your children, or if they aren't interested in knowing you, then you really need to work on your priorities.

If the preceding four paragraphs haven't made you feel guilty, then we suggest that you listen once again to "The Cat's in the Cradle."

There are few things that fathers regret more than losing their temper at the kids, but surprisingly it happens quite a bit.

Losing your temper serves no useful purpose. It doesn't make you more right, and it won't prove to be a successful motivator for your children. It actually weakens your negotiating position with your children. Even a kid knows that no one can be reasonable and angry at the same time. It boils down to this: If you want to maintain your authority and credibility with your child, then you'll have to learn to hold your anger. On those few occasions when you are correct, you can afford to keep your temper. On the more frequent times when you are wrong, you can't afford to lose it. Either way, anger doesn't do you any good.

If the preceding rationale doesn't inspire you to hold your temper, then at least follow these three tips for expressing your anger. If you have to do it, you might as well do it correctly so you don't hurt yourself:

ANGER EXPRESSION TIP #1

Keep the volume down. Avoid potential damage to your vocal chords. Besides, yelling actually accomplishes the opposite result that you want. The louder you yell, the less your kid is going to listen. We suggest that you express your anger by whispering. If for no other reason, your child will strain to hear you out of sheer curiosity.

ANGER EXPRESSION TIP # 2

Use few words. After your anger has subsided, you're going to have to retrieve all of the words that you spewed out during your rage. They might have been easy going out, but they are going to be difficult to swallow later. You'll save yourself a lot of choking if you simply pantomime your anger.

ANGER EXPRESSION TIP # 3

Forget counting to ten before you explode. Counting down is what they do before a rocket blasts off. We suggest saying a prayer instead. It might take supernatural assistance to control your temper, and God is the only One who can give it to you. If you have a particularly short temper, say a particularly long prayer.

IF YOU WANT TO MAINTAIN YOUR AUTHORITY AND CREDIBILITY WITH YOUR CHILD, THEN YOU'LL HAVE TO LEARN TO HOLD YOUR ANGER.

Your anger makes your mouth work at a faster rate than your mind. If you lose your temper, you are bound to say something to your child that you will regret. Hurtful words spoken in anger take a long time to heal. For the sake of your child, and yourself, learn to control your temper before it controls you.

9.4 AVERT YOUR GLANCE

Have you noticed how guys can see some things really well, while other everyday items never make it into their field of vision? We've never met a guy yet who can find the mayonnaise jar in the refrigerator without first yelling out, "Honey, where's the mayonnaise?" Of course, it's right there behind the half-eaten ham sandwich you put in there last week. Your wife can tell you this without even looking, and she can't understand why you can't see it, especially when you've been staring into the fridge for five minutes.[1]

Guys may lack vision for certain ordinary objects, but in other areas their eyesight is remarkably sharp. For example, guys can spot a TV tuned to ESPN in the back of any restaurant, even if it's in a different room. Guys can see a golf ball in the rough at a distance of 125 yards. They'll notice a Porsche 911 Carrera coming at them on the other side of a six-lane highway.

Such keen eyesight has its advantages, but it can also lead to problems, such as when a pretty woman walks anywhere near a guy. She can be coming from the back, the front, or even the side, and the average guy will pick up on the sight like an eagle spotting a brown mouse in a dirt field. When you were single, you could always use the excuse that you were "looking for the future Mrs. So-and-so." But now that you're married and a dad, checking out the chicks is not cool (even if you are good at disguising your furtive glances).

You might think you are getting away with a

harmless glance at a pretty woman—and this includes women in magazines, on television, or in underwear catalogs—but there's nothing harmless about inviting the wrong desires. Besides, most of the time your wife and kids know you're looking, and it doesn't do them any good either.

We're not suggesting that you wear blinders (although you might want to get rid of the mirrored sun glasses—you're not fooling anybody). All we're saying is that it's a good idea to look the other way when a Britney Spears wannabe struts by. Who knows? By averting your glance from this area where you are naturally gifted, you might get better at finding that mayonnaise jar.

[1] What she doesn't understand is that as a guy, you have a recessive gene that brings about "refrigerator blindness," "garbage blindness," and "your wife's new hairdo blindness."

WARNING SIGNS

Life is full of warning signs:

> The yellow flag at a NASCAR race can
> indicate a wreck up ahead.

> When you look down and can't see your feet,
> your stomach becomes its own prominent
> warning sign.

As a dad, you've got your own set of warning
signs. Here are a few that you should heed.

TROUBLE DADS WANT TO AVOID	THE WARNING SIGNS
9.1 Falling off the pedestal in the eyes of your children	Your children ask for a permanentmarker pen and sneak into your closet to deface your "No. 1 Dad" T-shirt. It now reads: "No. 11 Dad"
9.2 Spending too much time at work and not enough time with your child	Your kid calls your secretary to make an appointment with you.
9.3 Losing your temper too easily	You find ear plugs placed strategically around the house
9.4 Being attracted to other women	You enroll for a 6:00 A.M. aerobics class at an all-women's health club

9.5 FIX YOUR EYES

This world is full of dangerous distractions and potential potholes. Any guy who thinks he can navigate through the messy landscape on his own is only kidding himself. Any dad who thinks he can live a good life and be a better dad all alone is seriously deluded.

We all need help, and there's nothing wrong with asking for it. You aren't a weakling if you rely on some other faithful men to give you the encouragement and accountability you need to stay on the right path. In fact, any guy who gets around other spiritually mature men on a regular basis automatically gains the respect and admiration of his wife and kids. No one likes a loner, mainly because there's not much difference between a loner and a loser.

As much as we recommend that you join an accountability group of godly men, even that's not enough. You need to take another step in your quest to be a better dad. You need to find another role model.

The Bible tells us that there's only one person who lived a perfect, sinless life, and that's Jesus Christ. Not only did Jesus come to earth to die for our sins so we could have eternal life in heaven, but He **AS A DAD, YOUR SEARCH FOR THE PERFECT ROLE MODEL BEGINS AND ENDS WITH JESUS.** came to show us how to live right here and now on earth. Though He was God, Jesus knew what it was like to live as a man. He experienced all of the difficulties and temptations you will ever encounter, yet He overcame them without faltering.

As a dad, your search for the perfect role model begins and ends with Jesus. That's where you need to fix your eyes.

> *Let us fix our eyes on Jesus, the author and perfecter of our faith, who for the joy set before him endured the cross, scorning its shame, and sat down at the right hand of the throne of God. Consider him who endured such opposition from sinful men, so that you will not grow weary and lose heart (Hebrews 12:2-3, NIV).*

10

LEAVING A LEGACY

10.0 GUESTS IN YOUR HOME

There is going to come a time in your life when the child you love so much will leave your home. For many of us dads, this is a difficult thing to think about, not because we're afraid of what's going to happen to him or her, but because we're afraid of what's going to happen to us. How will we handle it?

A few years ago we found a quote from Henri Nouwen that helped us prepare for our own kids' departure, and we thought we'd pass it on to you:

> It indeed is hard to see our children leave after many years of much love and much work to bring them to maturity, but when we keep reminding ourselves that they are just guests who have their own destination, which we do not know or dictate, we might be more able to let them go in peace and with our blessing. A good host is not only able to receive his guests with honor and offer them all the care they need but also to let them go when their time to leave has come.[2]

WE DON'T OWN OUR KIDS; THEY ARE ON LOAN TO US FOR A WHILE.

You couldn't ask for better advice than that. As dads we need to keep our role in perspective. We don't own our kids; they are on loan to us for a while. They aren't ours to keep, but to prepare for a future in which they will build upon what they have learned from us. It's called a legacy, and it might just be the most important thing you will ever leave to your kids.

---

[2] Nouwen, Henri. Reaching Out. New York: Image Books, 1975, 83-84.

Ideally, the skills and techniques of being a good dad will be passed down from one generation to the next. Your grandfather taught your dad, your dad taught you, and you'll teach your son (or son-in-law). But passing on the skills of fatherhood is not like teaching a child how to drive a car. The instructional process is taught on an "as needed" basis. Your own dad is about twenty or thirty years ahead of you on the learning curve, so he'll be able to warn you about what's going to happen just before it occurs.

Maybe you are worried because there was a breakdown in the ancestral instruction process in your family:

Maybe you were raised in a family setting where your dad wasn't present;

Maybe you have been estranged from your father;

Maybe your father just wasn't a good role model;

Maybe your dad did a good job raising you, but he died before giving you any advice, and you didn't take notes while growing up.

Each of these circumstances is unfortunate, but you are not deprived of the presence of a Father who is anxious and able to give you guidance.

While your biological ancestry may be less than desirable, you can be extremely proud of your spiritual ancestry. You are a child of God, the Heavenly Father. God has everything that you could ever want in a Father:

> He knows everything. It is reassuring when you are seeking advice from a Heavenly Father who knows all.

> He is everywhere. Unlike many dads, your Heavenly Father is always around because He is everywhere at once. You never have to find Him. He is always available to you.

> He can do anything. When your kids are toddlers, they'll think the same thing about you, although that notion will be dispelled the first time they hear you wheezing when you bend down to tie your shoes. But your Heavenly Father is always able to handle your problems.

> He is loving and forgiving. Despite the fact that you might have been rebellious and disrespectful of Him, your Heavenly Father is anxious to have a personal relationship with you. But He is a perfect gentleman. He isn't going to force Himself on you. He is politely waiting for you to connect with Him.

DON'T WORRY IF YOU LACK A GOOD BIOLOGICAL FATHER FIGURE IN YOUR LIFE. YOU'VE GOT AN ANCESTRAL ADVANTAGE WITH YOUR HEAVENLY FATHER.

Don't worry if you lack a good biological father figure in your life. You've got an ancestral advantage with your Heavenly Father. If you rely on Him for your advice and guidance, you will be well equipped to be a great dad.

10.2 THE GREATEST LEGACY

Every dad leaves a legacy. There's no such thing as saying, "Well, I'm not too proud of who I am or what I've done, so I'm just going to skip that legacy deal." Even if you're a very private person, your legacy will live on in your children.

It's not that every detail of your life is going to be laid bare before your kids (thank goodness). Your legacy will be more about the way you lived and the way you influenced your children.

When it's all said and done, the greatest legacy you can leave is a life centered on God. In the Old Testament, here is what God told the children of Israel:

THE GREATEST LEGACY YOU CAN LEAVE IS A LIFE CENTERED ON GOD.

> *"Hear, O Israel! The Lord is our God, the Lord alone. And you must love the Lord your God with all your heart, all your soul, and all your strength. And you must commit yourselves wholeheartedly to these commands I am giving you today. Repeat them again and again to your children"* (Deuteronomy 6:4-7).

The same command applies to God's children today: We are to love God wholeheartedly and teach our children to do the same. That's the kind of legacy that will last for generations and please God into eternity.

— 10.3 KEEPING AND LETTING GO —

Being a dad is all about keeping and letting go. You keep your child for a while (about twenty years or so), and then it is time to let go. One isn't easier than the other. Both are delightful at times, and difficult at times. When you are in the middle of the first process, it is difficult to envision the next.

To keep a proper perspective on your role as the dad, we suggest that you reflect on the corporate adage that goes: Lead, follow, or get out of the way. With one small revision, that saying also applies to fatherhood. Notice how us dads need to accomplish all three actions:

Lead, follow *and* get out of the way.

Here is how it works:

LEAD

Be a leader of your children. Set the example for them to follow. This requires more than just advice. If you have any experience already as a dad, you know that children won't always follow what you say (often because they aren't listening). A good example has twice the value of good advice. Lead by example.

FOLLOW

If your children are going to follow in your footsteps, make sure you are walking down the right path. To do that, you must follow God's plan for your own life. This doesn't come automatically or naturally. You'll have to get to know who God is if you are going to follow Him.

GET OUT OF THE WAY

This is the best part. You will get to see your kids surpass your highest expectations (and theirs). As your kids go through the stages of childhood, your role as the dad takes the various forms of disciplinarian, coach, warden, mentor, and teacher. But as your child matures into adulthood, you will more likely be a friend and an admirer. Great dads allow their children to succeed. They know the difference between obstructing and observing, between interference and interest, and between meddling and mentoring. In other words, they know when to get out of the way.

Work on these three things. It will help your perspective while you are keeping your children, and it will help you when you are letting them go.

10.4 YOUR GREATEST JOY

Being a dad isn't an eighteen-year job assignment. It lasts a lot longer (and we aren't just referring to the fact that your child may move back home at age thirty). Once you take on the role of being a dad, it lasts for a lifetime. During that span of time, you will experience both good and bad events in the life of your child. The tragic things tend to fade in your memory, but you'll never forget the good moments (thanks to your wife snapping so many photos that annoyed everyone at the time). Those memorable occasions will include:

BIRTHDAYS
CHRISTMAS
VACATIONS
GRADUATIONS

SPORTING EVENTS
SCHOOL PROGRAMS
FAMILY GATHERINGS

You'll have fond memories of the good times you enjoyed with your children. But the activities of your child's life will never be as important as the quality of your child's character. If you want to experience real joy as a dad, then you must make every effort to develop your child into a man or woman of character. Each dimension of your child's life is important: physical, mental, emotional and spiritual. There is no easy way to accomplish this task. There is no quick fix. It will take your time, your energy and your resources. No job is more difficult, but no job is more rewarding.

We suspect that you are intimidated at the prospect of developing your child's character. You should be. We dads are fallible. How can we be expected to forge the character traits of our children when we have

difficulty determining the advantage of boxers over briefs? We shouldn't trust our children's future to our own instincts when those same instincts have gotten us into trouble.

Our only hope—and the only hope for our children—is dependence upon God for divine direction. If we want to instill principles of truth, hope, love, and justice in our children, we need to direct them to the One who is Truth, Hope, Love, and Justice. If our children are going to have any chance, they need to see God. We can help them see Him if we model His principles in our own lives.

THERE IS NO GREATER HONOR
THAN TO BE A DAD
BECAUSE YOU HAVE AN OPPORTUNITY TO
DIRECT YOUR CHILD IN TRUTH.

BUT THERE IS NO ASSIGNMENT MORE FRIGHTENING
THAN BEING A DAD
BECAUSE THAT OPPORTUNITY
IS YOUR RESPONSIBILITY.

AND WITH GOD'S HELP,
IF YOU ARE EVEN HALF WAY SUCCESSFUL AT THE TASK,
THERE IS NO ROLE MORE REWARDING
THAN BEING A DAD.

I could have no greater joy than to hear that my children live in the truth (3 John 4).

THE LAST WORD

If you are a dad,
we hope this book has been helpful to you.
Being a dad is a tough job,
but it's the best one any guy could have.

If you are wondering about our credentials,
we'll tell you right now that we don't have any.
But you can check us out at www.bruceandstan.com.

If you have always wanted to take a
cross-country road trip in a rental car,
You can live vicariously through our experience.
To make the trip tax-deductible, we wrote a few
books about it:

BRUCE & STAN SEARCH FOR THE MEANING OF LIFE
STORIES WE HEARD ABOUT COURAGE
STORIES WE HEARD ABOUT LOVE
STORIES WE HEARD ABOUT JOY
STORIES WE HEARD ABOUT HOPE

We are self-proclaimed non-experts, and
we have written about forty books that prove it.
Some of our other titles include:

WHAT TICKS GOD OFF
GOD SAID IT AND . . . BANG! IT HAPPENED
BRUCE & STAN'S GUIDE TO GOD
GOD IS IN THE SMALL STUFF

You can contact us by email at guide@bruceandstan.com.